TABLE-TALK OF SAMUEL ROGERS

SAMUEL ROGERS
1763-1855
from the chalk drawing by George Richmond R. A.

RECOLLECTIONS OF THE
TABLE-TALK OF
SAMUEL ROGERS

FIRST COLLECTED BY
THE REVD. ALEXANDER DYCE

———

Edited, with an Introduction, by
MORCHARD BISHOP

———

LONDON
THE RICHARDS PRESS LTD
MCMLII

INTRODUCTION

I

FOR every successful volume of Table Talk a happy accident is necessary: there must be the talker, and there must equally be the recorder. That is why such books are not common. It is notorious that Johnson's reputation as the greatest table-talker in English literature rests quite as much upon the assiduous and inspired note-taking of Boswell as upon the Doctor's powers as a conversationalist; and it is at least arguable that many of our wittiest talkers, such as Sydney Smith and Wilde, deprived themselves by their very brilliance of the posthumous reputations they would otherwise have enjoyed—-their audiences being so busy laughing that they were incapable of taking the necessary notes.

Indeed, with the notable exception of Boswell, and perhaps also of Hazlitt in the case of his *Conversations with Northcote*, it would really seem that the best recorders of the talk of other men are persons of a quiet and obscure turn, who are not in themselves apparently remarkable. Such was the Revd. Joseph Spence who, in his *Anecdotes*, preserved much of the conversation of Pope; such was Eckermann who so dexterously performed the same office for Goethe; such was Henry Nelson Coleridge, the nephew and son-in-law of Coleridge; and such, without question, was the Revd. Alexander Dyce, whose most entertaining *Recollections of the Table-talk of Samuel Rogers* is here, after an interval of many years, reprinted.

Dyce was an accomplished scholar, a massive, exact and courteous Scotsman, of whom, though he has not yet been dead a hundred years, few individual traces remain; apart, of course, from the valuable work that he did. He was born in George Street, Edinburgh, on June 30, 1798, the eldest son of a Lieutenant-General in the East India Company's service, and his mother was a Campbell. He was educated at Edinburgh High School and Exeter College, Oxford, whence, after obtaining his bachelor's degree in 1819, he took orders and embarked upon the career of curate, first at Lanteglos, near Fowey in Cornwall, and then at Nayland in Suffolk. He continued in this course for only three years and then he left the active service of the church and took to literature, settling down to a life of unremitting scholarship at No. 9, Gray's Inn Square. From 1825 until his death on May 15, 1869, he was principally engaged in editing a long series of reprints, mostly of the Elizabethan dramatists, Peele, Greene, Webster, Shirley, Middleton, Beaumont and Fletcher, Marlowe, and, in 1857, his *magnum opus*, the great nine-volume edition of Shakespeare. Nor was this all. He also edited the poems of Collins, Beattie, Pope, Akenside and Skelton, to say nothing of the learned works, in three volumes, of Richard Bentley; and, in 1856, applying to it the formidable powers of a mind which he had thus well sharpened upon the classics, the delightful and original little volume with which we are here concerned.

His was a useful if largely anonymous life, simple and remote from public affairs. His baggage for a week's visit, we are told, would consist of " seven shirts and a Sophocles "; and so great were his powers of concentration that he is himself reported to have observed, " If the conflagration of the universe were to take place to-morrow, I should not know that it was going on till the flames had reached Gray's Inn Gate." He was an incorrigible collector of books, pictures and prints, and at last, by 1859, his collection reached such proportions that he was literally forced by it out of his chambers and into more spacious premises at No. 33, Oxford Terrace. His books had overflowed everywhere, on to the floors and into the passages, until, as Forster remarks, " treasures of editions that would have deprived a bibliomaniac of his last remaining vestige of reason, were hidden away from all eyes, including his own ". It was, in fact, alleged that his library had become so unmanageable that he often found it simpler to go to the British Museum to consult a book, than to unearth from its lair his own copy of it.

In the last letter which, in June, 1868, Dyce sent to his friend John Forster, the biographer of Dickens, he comments appreciatively upon the new poem by a new young poet, *Atalanta in Calydon*, and he then goes on to make one of his very few personal references: " I suspect ", he wrote, " that I am very gradually dying, and if such is the case, I certainly have no reason to make any childish lamentation, for I have lived a great deal longer than most people who are born into this world, and I look back on my past existence without much disapprobation." With this cool and detached summing-up of a lifetime of patient and dedicated labour may perhaps fitly be coupled A. H. Bullen's valediction to Dyce, in the article that he wrote upon his career for the Dictionary of National Biography: " There have been editors more brilliant . . . but his deep and varied learning, his minute accuracy, and his nice discrimination have very rarely been equalled. So long as the best traditions of English scholarship survive, his name will be respected." It may be added that his great hoard of books and

pictures was bequeathed to South Kensington, where
the library catalogue alone of the Dyce Collection
comprises two formidable volumes.

So much for the begetter of one side of the book
that is before us: the recording half, in connection
with which Bullen's reference to " minute accuracy
and nice discrimination " should be particularly
noted, since, after the first publication of the *Table-talk*,
Dyce was most vigorously attacked on the score of
inaccuracy and exaggeration, both of them qualities
that were entirely foreign to his scrupulous method of
approach. Rogers had died on December 18, 1855,
and the *Table-talk* was out with astonishing celerity
being certainly before the public as early as February
14 the succeeding year. Yet despite this speedy
production, I believe the very rapidity of its appearance provides the best possible guarantee of its
authenticity, since it proves that Dyce did not compile
his book after the event, but really wrote down the
conversations as they occurred. His preface to
the first edition describes his method, and also reveals
the fact that Rogers knew what he was doing. Let
him then, in conclusion, speak for himself:

From my first introduction to Mr. Rogers, I was
in the habit of writing down, in all their minutiæ,
the anecdotes, &c. with which his conversation
abounded: and once on my telling him that I did so,
he expressed himself pleased,—the rather, perhaps,
because he sometimes had the mortification of
finding impatient listeners. Of those memoranda,
which gradually accumulated to a large mass, a
selection is contained in the following pages; the
subjects being arranged (as far as such miscellaneous
matter would admit of arrangement) under distinct
heads; and nothing having been inserted which
was likely to hurt the feelings of the living.

II

When we turn to the other side of the partnership—
to the talker, to Rogers himself, there is rather more to
be said. He was extremely ancient when he died, he
was, in fact, in his ninety-third year; and, though I
do not know when Dyce first met him (the earliest
recorded occasion of their being together that I have
seen occurs in Crabb Robinson's *Diary* under the date
August 28, 1849), he must have been a very old man
during the whole of the period that Dyce was making
his notes; and an old man whose memory, moreover,
was failing a little. There was, in addition, a further
factor to complicate matters. It will be noticed that,
as is customary with old people, the greater part of
the most vivid of his recollections relate to a time
many years before, when his own impressions were
themselves livelier. This, though natural enough, is
also partly due to the fact that Rogers himself, at a
very much earlier period of his life, had contracted the
habit of noting down on paper the substance of the
conversations that he had enjoyed with men he
admired; with men who, with a couple of exceptions,
had all for a long time been dead. These same notes,
under the title of *Recollections by Samuel Rogers*, were, in
the year 1859, published in the very fragmentary form
in which he had left them, by his nephew and literary
executor, Samuel Sharpe; and it may, I fancy, be
presumed that it was the publication (and the success)
of Dyce's book that inspired the production of this
other much inferior, though doubtless equally authentic,
volume. In this work the conversations were grouped
under the names of the speakers, and consisted of the
utterances of Fox, Burke, Grattan, Porson, Horne
Tooke, Talleyrand, Erskine, Scott, Grenville and

Wellington. With the exception of some of the sayings of the Duke of Wellington, most of the best of these observations already occur, in one form or another, in Dyce's earlier collection. It is, I think, almost certain that he had had access to the manuscript of this later book, which it is known Rogers was in the habit of lending to his friends.

I refer here to this other volume because, in 1903, Mr. G. H. Powell, in the latest edition of the *Table-talk* to be published, took upon himself to produce a book wherein was blended what he considered to be the best of Dyce's material together with a selection of items from the 1859 *Recollections*. I have not in the following pages adopted this method. The 1859 book is an interesting little volume; but it is not a very readable one. Dyce's is an immensely readable one, and it has been put together with a good deal of carefully contrived and concealed art.

Even so, I should not wish to give the reader the impression that the pages which follow are a verbatim reprint of Dyce's original text. This is not so. There are some pages, not many but some, which to the taste of the present time have lost their savour. For the most part they consist of such things as quotations from Rogers's own works, or from the works of other writers, such as Crowe, who are now not much admired. These pages I have omitted, and to make up to some extent for such omissions I have imported into the body of the book a number of the more entertaining anecdotes concerning Richard Porson which Dyce included in his volume but under a separate heading, *Porsoniana*, since they were not given to him by Rogers, but by Rogers's life-long friend, William Maltby, a solicitor who in 1809 succeeded Porson as Librarian to the London Institution. For this arbitrary handling of an original text, I hope I may be forgiven. I have thus handled it on the grounds that, as the book was in the first instance intended to amuse, the removal of what in the process of time has ceased to be amusing may still be defended as a true extension of the wishes of its original compiler.

One word, too, is necessary on the matter of the footnotes. Those that are here printed without comment are Dyce's. Some that were supplied by Maltby are so noted; and those for which I am myself responsible I have marked *Ed.* In an Appendix at the end are included a handful of anecdotes which Dyce, for one reason or another, suppressed when his book was in proof. The text is based upon the second edition of 1856.

III

And now, having dealt with Dyce and with what is, I suppose, his most original, though not perhaps his most valuable, feat of editing, we come at length to the heart of the matter: to the consideration of that strange, rather repellent, more than half-forgotten figure whose gossip is here set down for our entertainment: to Samuel Rogers, the only English writer, so far as I am aware, who combined in one lifetime the somewhat disparate arts of banking and of poetry. It would be idle to pretend that Rogers is a figure of importance, or one whose works literary fashion will some day rediscover. His poetry—and I have read most of it before considering myself entitled to make such a statement—is dead beyond much hope of resurrection. There was never a great deal of it, and it is one of the lasting miracles of literary history that upon so scanty a foundation he should have been able to rear so lofty a reputation. How this came about is, indeed, very much more interesting than the poetry itself. It is as a social portent that Rogers must chiefly concern us to-day; and as such a portent he is still, I think, remarkable.

His remarkableness, I may say, rests chiefly on the fact that there would seem to be hardly any figure in recent literature to whom may be found so many contemporary references which yet yield so little. Rogers knew everybody, and none of the memoirs of his time are without copious references to him. And yet, strangely enough, these references tell us next to nothing about him. There is the façade, of course, the impeccable house in St. James's Place with its Flaxman mantelpieces, its Giorgione *Knight* and its Bellini *Doge*; there are the literary breakfasts; there are the carefully prepared impromptu witticisms: but one may seek in vain behind this façade for the figure of the real man. After his death, and after the publication of Dyce's book and the *Recollections*, there was a longish period of silence before, in 1887-9, a Mr. P. W. Clayden, at the behest of the executors, deposited upon Rogers's memory three large and heavy volumes that were based upon his own papers and entitled, respectively, *The Early Life of Samuel Rogers* and *Rogers and his Contemporaries* in two volumes. These tomes, which are crammed with very carefully ' edited ' original documents, are dedicated, for the most part, to the laudable end of demonstrating that Rogers was a virtuous and benevolent man, an important literary figure, a representative Dissenter and Whig. As a slight corrective to this impressive canonisation, a few acid references to him are to be found in Greville, in Creevey, in Carlyle, and in the *Memoirs* of Harriet Martineau, to say nothing of an exceedingly savage lampoon by Byron, if Byron in his most mordant vein may be taken as evidence. Some of these references I shall cite in more detail later;

but before doing so I think it may be desirable to give here a short outline of the banker-poet's career.

He was born on July 30, 1763, at Newington Green, Middlesex, which was then a real Green, with ancient elms and Elizabethan houses clustered around it. His father, Thomas Rogers, was of mixed Welsh and French ancestry, the son of a glass manufacturer of Stourbridge in Worcestershire, who had married his master's daughter. This lady, Mary Radford, was of radical and nonconformist stock; and her husband, who had originally been a Tory, upon marriage adopted her views, and, shortly after his arrival in London, became a banker with premises upon Cornhill. Young Rogers was educated at an academy at Stoke Newington, and attended the Presbyterian chapel there which was presided over by Dr. Richard Price, a divine of so overwhelming a personality that the boy's first notion of a career was to follow his example and enter the ministry. But he was a delicate child, and his father had other views for him; between the ages of sixteen and seventeen he was put into the family bank. By the time he was one-and-twenty he was a partner in the concern, receiving ten sixty-eighths of the profits.

He had, however, from an early age nourished literary aspirations. Dr. Price was a prolific author, though his works were for the most part on such recondite topics as *The Effect of the Aberration of Light on the Time of the Transit of Venus*, or *Calculations* (for an insurance company) *on the Expectation of Life;* while in the very next pew to that which the Rogers' occupied in his chapel there sat a girl who was later to be celebrated as Mary Wollstonecraft; and some one hundred years earlier the great Daniel Defoe had worshipped in the same tabernacle. Such influences could not be gainsaid: by the time he was eighteen,

Rogers had already contributed essays to the *Gentleman's Magazine*, and shortly after this he composed a comic opera called *The Vintage of Burgundy*, in the course of which his heroine was pursued by her lover in the guise, then deemed highly poetical, of an organgrinder. At three-and-twenty he published his first poem, which somewhat resembled Gray's *Bard* and was entitled *An Ode to Superstition;* or, rather, it would be more accurate to say that he paid Cadell thirty pounds to publish it. This, from Cadell's point of view, was just as well, since by the end of four years only twenty copies of the work had been sold. Soon after this he contributed a poem, *On a Tear*, to *The World*, the organ of the Della Cruscans.

But Rogers was never a prolific poet, and since no one nowadays is likely to take an ardent interest in his poems, I think the best way in which I can deal with them here is by reproducing an extraordinarily revealing little table concerning them, which the poet himself set out as an entry in his Commonplace Book, thus:—

Date of completion	Poem	Time for composition and revision	Age of author at completion
1785	Ode to Superstition	2 years	22
1792	Pleasures of Memory	7 years	29
1798	Epistle to a Friend	6 years	35
1812	Columbus	14 years	49
1813	Jacqueline	1 year	50
1819	Human Life	6 years	56
1834	Italy	15 years	71

To this table should just be added the fact that, with the exception of his *Jacqueline* which was published jointly with Byron's *Lara*, Rogers in each case followed the method which he had employed with his earliest poem, and himself paid the expenses of publication.

Such a table as this is one that can hardly be contemplated without being put in mind of Sydney Smith's not unjustified witticism: " When Rogers produces a couplet, he goes to bed, and the knocker is tied up, and straw is laid down, and the caudle is made, and the answer to enquiries is, that Mr. Rogers is as well as can be expected." And, indeed, little need be said now of these works which, in Hazlitt's words, have " nothing like truth of nature, or simplicity of expression "; in proof of which he goes on to refer to Rogers's description, in his *Epistle to a Friend*, of that friend's ice-house, " in which Mr. Rogers has carried the principle of elegant evasion and delicate insinuation of his meaning so far, that the Monthly Reviewers mistook his friend's ice-house for a dog-kennel ". Nevertheless, *The Pleasures of Memory* gauged the taste of the time to a nicety; it said nothing much, but it said it very smoothly, with the result that, by 1816, nineteen editions of it had been sold. As for *Columbus*, the last word may safely be left with Wordsworth: on being asked for his opinion of it, he replied, with crushing ambiguity: " Columbus is what you meant it to be." *Human Life* is perhaps the most readable of the longer flights, though even this Miss Mitford described as " one of those sort of poems which are very short and seem very long "; and *Italy* is certainly the most sustained and ambitious of them all. It must not, moreover, be forgotten that *Italy*, in the sumptuous Turner-illustrated edition which the author produced at a cost to himself of some £7,335 after the earlier, unillustrated (and anonymous) editions had proved a total failure (" It would have been dished," said Luttrell " but for the plates "), was the work that first directed the juvenile Ruskin's lively mind towards the scenery and architecture of Italy. There are, indeed, some good things in *Italy*, if one is prepared to dig for them, though most of them, oddly enough, are in prose. There is, pre-eminently, the famous note on Raphael's *Transfiguration*, upon which Rogers is reputed to have worked ceaselessly for a fortnight:

' You admire that picture,' said an old Dominican to me at Padua, as I stood contemplating a Last Supper in the Refectory of his Convent, the figures as large as the life. ' I have sat at my meals before it for seven and forty years; and such are the changes that have taken place among us—so many have come and gone in the time—that, when I look upon the company there—upon those who are sitting at that table, silent as they are—I am some-times inclined to think that we, and not they, are the shadows '. . . .

But when all is said and done, these poems have had their day and have achieved the purpose for which they were written. In conjunction with his wealth (even as early as 1788 Rogers's income was estimated at about £5,000 a year), they procured for him what he most desired: his entry into the best society, both literary and aristocratic. From 1803, when he moved into his celebrated house at No. 22, St. James's Place, up to the day of his death, Rogers was the self-appointed dictator of English letters, the " Oracle of Holland House " in Macaulay's phrase; and, on the whole, he used his great powers not unworthily. He was an adept at composing quarrels; he ended the differences of Moore and Jeffrey, of Byron and Moore, of Dr. Parr and Mackintosh; he helped in their financial difficulties Sheridan and Wordsworth and Sir Thomas Lawrence, as well as countless others, not least that last bright relic of the Sheridan charm, the luckless Caroline Norton. Everyone who made any sort of hit in the literary sense was honoured by an invitation to his breakfasts; it became, as it were, the seal of success; from Wordsworth and Coleridge up to Dickens, Thackeray and Tennyson he knew everybody, and his house was particularly a Mecca to literary visitors from America. One of the most surprising names among those who were furnished with an introduction to him was that of the sultry creator of Captain Ahab, Herman Melville.

But before we utterly abandon Rogers as a poet, and turn to the social life that was his real claim to distinction, is it quite impossible to find in all his collected works any lines that serve a little to justify his pretensions? I think we may do so in at least two cases. There are, first, the touching verses that he wrote as an epitaph on the robin-redbreast of Miss Johnes of Hafod:

> Tread lightly here, for here, 'tis said,
> When piping winds are hushed around,
> A small note wakes from underground,
> Where now his tiny bones are laid.
> No more in lone and leafless groves,
> With ruffled wing and faded breast,
> His friendless, homeless spirit roves;
> —Gone to the world where birds are blest!
> Where never cat glides o'er the green,
> Or school-boy's giant form is seen;
> But Love, and Joy, and smiling Spring
> Inspire their little souls to sing!

Really, well-known as it is, it is charming; and then, far less well-known are the brief lines called *Captivity*, which Hookham Frere compared to a Greek epigram, and which I myself think, written by Rogers's own account as early as his 'teens, is a most unexpected

forerunner of so pre-Raphaelite a matter as Tennyson's
Mariana:

> Caged in old woods, whose reverend echoes wake
> When the hern screams along the distant lake,
> Her little heart oft flutters to be free,
> Oft sighs to turn the unrelenting key.
> In vain! the nurse that rusted relic wears,
> Nor moved by gold—nor to be moved by tears;
> And terraced walls their black reflection throw
> On the green-mantled moat that sleeps below.

Such lines were not very common as early as the
1780's; they seem almost to be the first stirrings of the
great wind that was to blow through *Christabel* and
Kubla Khan.

IV

The revenges of time are curious and comprehensive.
Rogers, who had made quite a business of levering
Wordsworth's rugged frame into his own exiguous
court-suit upon such occasions as the poet laureate
was obliged to attend at Court in his official capacity,
was, at his old friend's death in 1850, and when he
was himself already eighty-seven, offered, by Prince
Albert's own royal hands, the laureateship. He had,
upon reflection, the sense to refuse it, and when Lord
John Russell then requested him to report upon the
" character and position " of Mr. Alfred Tennyson,
his observations were so favourable that it was not
long before Moxon, the publisher, was engaged in
tugging Tennyson into that same court-suit of Rogers's
which had earlier graced the limbs of Wordsworth.
Such, just a century ago, was Rogers's poetical reputation, of which so little now remains. And that is

where the revenges of time come into the picture: for, just as his poetry is dead, so I believe that this little book of his table-talk, which he never read and never saw, is abundantly alive; and alive in a way in which his own fragmentary *Recollections* are not. If Rogers is to be remembered at all by posterity, I think it will be because of this volume. There are unforgettable things in it: there is Fox glancing moodily out of the windows of the Louvre in October, 1802, and remarking that the hot sun will burn up his turnips at St. Anne's Hill; there is the inimitable observation of the Duke of Wellington, on being informed that the ship he is in is sinking: " Then I shall not take off my boots "; there is the famous account of the Wordsworth-Coleridge tour of Scotland " in a vehicle that looked very like a cart "; there are half a hundred things as good, anecdotes most veracious and characteristic of Byron and Scott, of Horne Tooke and Beckford, of Pitt and Fox and Sheridan.

All, you perceive, matters concerning other people. There is scarcely a word here that gives us any picture of Rogers himself, save indeed in the days of his extreme youth. And there, I think, we stumble upon his secret. For all the pomp and splendour of his social life, he was a shy man and a frightened man, one who knew all too well the extreme thinness of his own talent. Byron, I fancy, as early as 1813 and long before they had fallen out, sensed as much when he wrote in his diary: " Rogers is silent, and, it is said, severe. When he does talk, he talks well; and on all subjects of taste his delicacy of expression is as pure as his poetry. If you enter his house, his drawing-room, his library, you of yourself say, ' This is not the dwelling of a common mind.' There is not a gem, a coin, a book thrown aside on his chimney-piece, his sofa, his table, that does not bespeak an almost fastidious

elegance in the possessor. But this very delicacy must
be the misery of his existence. Oh the jarrings his
disposition must have encountered through life!"
Perhaps the jarrings were not entirely brought about
by fastidiousness; for, at any rate, one thing is clear:
he clung with desperation to the utterances of men
greater than himself, noting them and remembering
them as if only through them might he attain his own
passport to immortality. It was notorious that he
had a very weak voice, and once when he was asked
by Sir Henry Taylor why he said such ill-natured
things, he replied that if he did not say ill-natured
things no one at all would hear what he said. In
similar style, another wit remarked of him that he made
his way in the world as Hannibal had made his across
the Alps—with vinegar; and Harriet Martineau went
so far as to observe: "His causticity was his pass-key
everywhere. Except the worship paid to the Railway
King for his wealth, we know of nothing in modern
society so extraordinary and humiliating as the
deference paid to Rogers for his ill-nature." He did
emit, without doubt, quantities of the most ill-natured
observations, from a large proportion of which the wit
has now evaporated, though some are still amusing.
One instance is his dictum that it doesn't matter whom
a man marries, he is sure to find the next morning
that he has married someone else; another is his reply
to the gentleman who complained that, if open seats
replaced pews in church, he might find himself sitting
next to his own coachman: "So you might in
Heaven!" But, very fortunately for us, he did not
permit his own peculiarities to interfere with his
records of the utterances of others. He was, in his
own curious way, even something of a hero-worshipper,
though it would appear that most of his heroes were
men of action and men of affairs, rather than men of

letters. The list that has already been given of the persons whose conversation he thought it worth while to preserve in writing demonstrates this, since, except for Scott and Porson, none of them were literary men; and Porson was a scholar, and Scott a quite exceptional case.

It is, therefore, all the more curious that it should be the men of affairs who, on the whole, give us the least attractive picture of Rogers. Greville did not like him, though he found his breakfasts highly agreeable; and so he goes out of his way to draw a most curious parallel between Moore and Rogers: the poetry of the former (he says) being " so licentious, that of the latter so pure; much of its popularity owing to its being so carefully weeded of everything approaching to indelicacy; and the contrast between the *lives* and *works* of the two men—the former a pattern of conjugal and domestic regularity, the latter of all the men he had ever known the greatest sensualist." Creevey is even more severe: " What a sour snarling beast this Rogers is, and such a fellow for talking about the grandees he lives with—*female* as well as male, and the loves he has upon his hands. Sefton and I hold him a damned bore." Or again there is Carlyle, quite up to his usual form: " A most sorrowful, distressing, distracted old phenomenon, hovering over the rim of deep eternities with nothing but light babble, fatuity, vanity, and the frostiest London wit in his mouth. Sometimes I felt as if I could throttle him, the poor old wretch! " Byron's strictures are still more widely known: Rogers was very much his friend at the time of the separation, but it is apparent from Byron's letters to Murray that, thereafter, he talked too much, with the result that Byron later composed, in September, 1820, the quite devastating lines to which no one ever heard Rogers refer, though there

INTRODUCTION

was no doubt that he knew all about them, since they
were published in *Fraser's Magazine* as early as 1833.
Couched in the form of a riddle, they are familiar;
but since they conclude, as it were, the case for the
prosecution, they had perhaps better be given here.
Besides, they are incomparably vivid, and give, I am
afraid, an admirable picture of the exterior present-
ment of Rogers; of that cadaverous Rogers to whom
Lord Alvanley is alleged to have remarked on one
occasion: " Rogers, as you can afford it, why don't
you set up your hearse? " Clayden, I may remark,
in the official biography makes himself extremely
ridiculous about these lines, which, as he cannot
explain them away, he is obliged to pretend no one,
not even Rogers, ever took seriously. As pure invective
they are, I must confess, very enjoyable:

QUESTION

Nose and chin would shame a knocker,
Wrinkles that would puzzle Cocker;
Mouth which marks the envious scorner,
With a scorpion in each corner,
Turning its quick tail to sting you,
In the place that most may wring you;
Eyes of lead-like hue, and gummy;
Carcase picked out from some mummy;
Bowels (but they were forgotten,
Save the liver, and that's rotten);
Skin all sallow, flesh all sodden—
From the Devil would frighten God in.
Is't a corpse stuck up for show,
Galvanised at times to go?
With the Scripture in connexion,
New proof of the resurrection?
Vampire, ghost, or ghoul, what is it?
I would walk ten miles to miss it.

ANSWER

Many passengers arrest one,
To demand the same free question.
Shorter's my reply, and franker—
That's the Bard, the Beau, the Banker.
Yet if you could bring about,
Just to turn him inside out,
Satan's self would seem less sooty,
And his present aspect—Beauty.
Mark that (as he marks the bilious
Air so softly supercilious)
Chastened bow, and mock humility,
Almost sickened to servility;
Hear his tone (which is to talking
That which creeping is to walking:
Now on all-fours, now on tip-toe);
Hear the tales he lends his lips to;
Little hints of heavy scandals;
Every friend in turn he handles;
All which women, or which men do,
Glides forth in an innuendo,
Clothed in odds and ends of humour—
Herald of each paltry rumour,
From divorces down to dresses,
Women's frailties, men's excesses,
All which life presents of evil
Makes for him a constant revel.
You're his foe, for that he fears you,
And in absence blasts and sears you;
You're his friend, for that he hates you,
First caresses, and then baits you;
Darting on the opportunity
When to do it with impunity.
You are neither—then he'll flatter
Till he finds some trait for satire;

Hunts your weak point out, then shows it
Where it injures to disclose it,
In the mode that's most invidious,
Adding every trait that's hideous,
From the bile whose black'ning river
Rushes through his Stygian liver.
Then he thinks himself a lover—
Why, I really can't discover,
In his mind, eye, face, or figure;
Viper-broth might give him vigour;
Let him keep the cauldron steady,
He the venom has already.
For his faults—he has but *one*—
'Tis but envy, when all's done.
He but pays the pain he suffers;
Clipping, like a pair of snuffers,
Lights which ought to burn the brighter
For this temporary blighter.
He's the cancer of his species:
And will eat himself to pieces,
Plague personified, and famine;
Devil, whose sole delight is damning!

For his merits, would you know 'em?
Once he wrote a pretty poem.

It is a brilliant if a terrifying picture, and I think the
only thing to be said about it here is to suggest that it
may well be studied in juxtaposition with Rogers's own
not uncharitable references to Byron which are set
down hereafter, and which were of course made to
Dyce long after Rogers had become familiar with his
noble friend's murderous portrait of himself.

Final judgments, however, are not easy to make;
nor in any case is one demanded in this place.
Rogers's remarks to Mme. de Staël on Campbell,

which occur in the text that follows, have been quoted very often as a proof of his crass insensibility, yet his generosity to this fellow-author, and to others that were in trouble, was a byword; and Campbell himself said of him: "Borrow £500 of Rogers, and he will never say a word against you until you want to repay him." He was everlastingly assisting Moore with money, and Crabbe with advice, and his benevolences to obscure bards who were also basket-weavers and so forth were open and notorious. He was also, at any rate in his later years, very fond of children, to whom he was in the habit of giving elaborate Twelfth Night parties, in the course of which he would demonstrate electrical machines, do conjuring-tricks, play on the hurdy-gurdy, and let off fireworks. His influence on the taste of his time in the matter of the visual arts was sound even if not particularly progressive, as might have been expected in one who had spanned the enormous gulf between the founding of the Academy and the rise of John Ruskin. We have heard a good deal of how the people who did not like him regarded him, and so it is only fair to close the record with the testimonies of some of his friends. Lord Holland's couplet upon his accustomed seat in the summer-house at Holland House is well known, and remains the neatest possible tribute to the author of *The Pleasures of Memory*:

Here Rogers sat, and here for ever dwell
To me, those pleasures that he sings so well.

Less familiar is the robust compliment that his old competitor, Sydney Smith, paid him in a letter to Lady Holland, who had come across him by accident in Rome. "Show me," he wrote, "a more kind and friendly man; . . . one from good manners,

knowledge, fun, taste, and observation, more agreeable;
. . . a man of more strict political integrity, and of
better character in private life. If I were to choose
any Englishman in foreign parts whom I should wish
to blunder upon, it should be Rogers." And perhaps
it may be left to the unfortunate Mrs. Caroline Norton,
whom he had so staunchly and steadfastly befriended
from the very start of her many troubles, to have the
last word: " He was (she said, describing him in
extreme old age) the very embodiment of quiet, from
his voice to the last harmonious little picture that hung
in his lulled room; and a curious figure he seemed—
an elegant pale watch-tower, showing for ever what
a quiet port literature and the fine arts might offer, in
an age of ' progress ', when everyone is tossing,
struggling, wrecking, and foundering on a sea of
commercial speculation or political adventure; where
people fight even over pictures, and if a man does buy
a picture, it is with a burning desire to prove it is a
Raphael to his yelping enemies, rather than to point it
out with a slow white finger to his breakfasting friends."

So to the last, I think, he remains an enigma; a man,
like the rest of us, who had friends who loved, and
enemies who hated, him; a man whom it is not
possible for posterity to like very much, but whom it is
still possible to respect; and to whom it is even easier
to be grateful for the alms for oblivion which, in the
pages that follow, he has preserved for our lasting
entertainment. Dyce, I fancy, did for him what he
was never able to do for himself: he erected for him a
safe niche within which he may enjoy the plaudits of
future generations without any of that fear of being
found out which made his life on earth such a
laboriously cautious, fussily active, carefully contrived
affair.

M.B.

RECOLLECTIONS OF THE
TABLE-TALK OF SAMUEL ROGERS

I was taught by my mother, from my earliest
infancy, to be tenderly kind towards the meanest
living thing; and, however people may laugh,
I sometimes very carefully put a stray gnat or
wasp out at the window.—My friend Lord
Holland, though a kind-hearted man, does not
mind killing flies and wasps; he says, " I have
no feeling for *insects*."—When I was on the
Continent with Richard Sharp,* we one day
observed a woman amusing her child by holding
what we at first thought was a mouse tied to a
string, with which a cat was playing. Sharp
was all indignation at the sight; till, on looking
more closely, he found that the supposed mouse
was a small rat; upon which he exclaimed,
" Oh, I have no pity for *rats!* "—People choose
to give the term *vermin* to those animals that
happen to like what they themselves like;
wasps eat peaches, and they call them vermin.—
I can hardly persuade myself that there is no
compensation in a future existence for the
sufferings of animals in the present life,—for

* Richard Sharp (1759–1835), generally known as " Conversation
Sharp." One of Rogers's best friends, he was a hatter and a patron
of the arts. Wordsworth said of him that he knew Italy better than
anyone he had ever met.—*Ed*.

instance, when I see a horse in the streets unmercifully flogged by its brutal driver.

I well remember one of the heads of the rebels upon a pole at Temple-Bar,—a black shapeless lump. Another pole was bare, the head having dropt from it.*

In my childhood, after doing any thing wrong, I used always to feel miserable from a consciousness of having done it: my parents were quite aware of this, and therefore seldom reproved me for a fault,—leaving me to reprove myself.

When I was about thirteen, my father and mother gave a great children's ball, at which many grown-up folks were also present. I was dancing a minuet with a pretty little girl; and at the moment when I ought to have put on my hat and given both hands to my partner, I threw the hat among the young ladies who were sitting on benches, and so produced great surprise and confusion in the room. This strange feat was occasioned by my suddenly recollecting a story of some gallant youth who had signalised himself in the same way.

In my boyhood, my father one day called me

* " The last heads which remained on the Bar were those of Fletcher and Townley. ' Yesterday,' says a news-writer of the 1st of April 1772, ' one of the rebels' heads on Temple Bar fell down. There is only one head now remaining.' " P. Cunningham's *Handbook of London*, sub *Temple-Bar*.

and my brothers into his room, and asked us each what professions we wished to follow. When my turn came, I said (to my father's annoyance) that I should like " to be a preacher "; for it was then the height of my ambition to figure in a pulpit;—I thought there was nothing on earth so *grand*. This predilection, I believe, was occasioned chiefly by the admiration I felt for Dr. Price* and for his preaching. He was our neighbour (at Newington Green), and would often drop in, to spend the evening with us, in his dressing-gown: he would talk, and read the Bible, to us, till he sent us to bed in a frame of mind as heavenly as his own. He lived much in the society of Lord Lansdowne and other people of rank; and his manners were extremely polished. In the pulpit he was great indeed,— making his hearers forget the *preacher* and think only of the *subject*.

My father belonged originally to the Church of England; but, soon after his marriage with my mother (a very handsome and very amiable woman), he withdrew from it at her persuasion, and became one of Dr. Price's hearers.

When I was a school-boy, I wore, like other school-boys, a cocked hat;—we used to run about the fields, chasing butterflies, in cocked hats. After growing up, I have walked through St. Paul's Churchyard in a cocked hat.

* Richard Price, minister of the Presbyterian Chapel attended by Rogers in his youth at Stoke Newington. He was a vigorous Whig and an associate of Dr. Priestley.—*Ed*.

I saw Garrick act only once,—the part of Ranger in *The Suspicious Husband*. I remember that there was a great crowd, and that we waited long in a dark passage of the theatre, on our way to the pit. I was then a little boy. My father had promised to take me to see Garrick in Lear; but a fit of the mumps kept me at home.

Before his going abroad, Garrick's attraction had much decreased; Sir William Weller Pepys said that the pit was often almost empty. But, on his return to England, people were mad about seeing him; and Sir George Beaumont and several others used frequently to get admission into the pit, before the doors were opened to the public, by means of bribing the attendants, who bade them " be sure, as soon as the crowd rushed in, to pretend to be in a great heat, and to wipe their faces, as if they had just been struggling for entrance."

Jack Bannister told me, that one night he was behind the scenes of the theatre when Garrick was playing Lear; and that the tone in which Garrick uttered the words, " O fool, I shall go mad! " absolutely thrilled him.

Garrick used to pay an annual visit to Lord Spencer at Althorp; where, after tea, he generally entertained the company by reading scenes from Shakespeare. Thomas Grenville, who met him there, told me that Garrick would steal anxious glances at the faces of his audience, to perceive what effect his reading produced; that, one night, Garrick observed a lady listening to him very attentively, and yet never moving a muscle of her countenance; and that, speaking of her next day, he said, " She seems a very worthy person; but I hope that—that—that she won't be present at my reading to-night."—Another evening at Althorp, when Garrick was about to exhibit some particular stage-effect of which they had been talking, a young gentleman got up and placed the candles upon the floor, that the light might be thrown on his face as from the lamps in the theatre. Garrick, displeased at his officiousness, immediately sat down again.

My friend Maltby* and I, when we were very young men, had a strong desire to see Dr. Johnson; and we determined to call upon him and introduce ourselves. We accordingly proceeded to his house in Bolt Court; and I had my hand on the knocker, when our courage failed us, and we retreated. Many years afterwards, I mentioned this circumstance to Boswell, who said, " What a pity that you did not go boldly in! he would have received you with all kindness."

Dr. Johnson said to an acquaintance of mine, " My other works are wine and water; but my *Rambler* is pure wine." The world now thinks differently.

Lady Spencer recollected Johnson well, as she used to see him often in her girlhood. Her mother, Lady Lucan, would say, " Nobody dines with us to-day; therefore, child, we'll go and get Dr. Johnson." So they would drive to Bolt Court, and bring the doctor home with them.

At the sale of Dr. Johnson's books, I met General Oglethorpe, then very, very old, the flesh of his face looking like parchment. He amused us youngsters by talking of the alterations that had been made in London and of the great additions it had received within his recollection. He said that he had shot snipes in Conduit-Street!

By the by, General Fitzpatrick remembered the time when St. James's Street used to be crowded with the carriages of the ladies and gentlemen who were walking in the Mall,—the ladies with their heads in full dress, and the gentlemen carrying their hats under their arms. The proprietors of Ranelagh and Vauxhall used to send decoy-ducks among them, that is, persons attired in the height of fashion, who every now and then would exclaim in a very audible tone, " What charming weather for Ranelagh " or " for Vauxhall! "

Ranelagh was a very pleasing place of amusement. There persons of inferior rank mingled with the highest nobility of Britain. All was so orderly and still, that you could hear the *whishing* sound of the ladies' trains, as the immense assembly walked round and round the room. If you chose, you might have tea, which was served up in the neatest equipage possible.

The price of admission was half-a-crown. People generally went to Ranelagh between nine and ten o'clock.

My first attempt at authorship was a series of papers headed *The Scribbler*,* which appeared in *The Gentleman's Magazine*,—for what year I forget. I have never looked at them since: I daresay they are sad trash.

The first poetry I published was the *Ode to Superstition*, in 1786. I wrote it while I was in my teens, and afterwards touched it up.† I paid down to the publisher thirty pounds to insure him from being a loser by it. At the end of four years, I found that he had sold about twenty copies. However, I was consoled by reading in a critique on the Ode that I was " an able writer," or some such expression.—The short copy of verses entitled *Captivity* was also composed when I was a very young man. It was a favourite with Hookham Frere, who said that it resembled a Greek epigram.

My lines *To the Gnat*, which some of the reviewers laughed at, were composed in consequence of my *sufferings* from the attacks of that insect while I lived at Newington Green. My eyes used to be absolutely swollen-up with gnat-bites. I awoke one morning in that condition when I was engaged to spend the day at

* *The Scribbler* extends to eight Numbers,—in *The Gentleman's Magazine* for 1781, pp. 68, 119, 168, 218, 259, 306, 355, 405 (mis-paged 409).

† According to a note in Mr. R.'s collected poems, it was " written in 1785."

Streatham with Mr. and Mrs. Piozzi, to meet Miss Farren* (afterwards Lady Derby); and it was only by the application of laudanum to my *wounds* that I was enabled to keep my engagement. Nothing could exceed the elegance and refinement of Miss Farren's appearance and manners.

People have taken the trouble to write my *Life* more than once; and strange assertions they have made both about myself and my works. In one biographical account it is stated that I submitted *The Pleasures of Memory* in manuscript to the critical revision of Richard Sharp: now, when that poem was first published, I had not yet formed an acquaintance with Sharp (who was introduced to me by the oldest of my friends, Maltby). The beautiful lines, " Pleasures of Memory!—oh, supremely blest," &c., which I have inserted in a note on Part Second, were composed by a Mr. Soame, who died in India in 1803, at which time he was a lieutenant in the dragoons. I believe that he destroyed himself. I had heard that the lines were in a certain newspaper, and went to Peel's Coffee-house to see that paper: there I first read them, and there I transcribed them.

On the publication of *The Pleasures of Memory*, I sent a copy to Mason, who never acknowledged it. I learned, however, from Gilpin,† and to my great satisfaction, that Mason, in a letter to him, had spoken well of it;—he pronounced it to be

---

* Elizabeth Farren, the actress, whom Lord Derby married in May, 1797, some seven weeks after the death of his previous wife.—*Ed*.

† The Rev. William Gilpin, vicar of Boldre in the New Forest, who wrote and illustrated numerous works on English scenery.—*Ed*.

very different in style from the poetry of the day.

During my whole life I have borne in mind the speech of a woman to Philip of Macedon; " I appeal from Philip drunk to Philip sober." After writing any thing in the excitement of the moment, and being greatly pleased with it, I have always put it by for a day or two; and then carefully considering it in every possible light, I have altered it to the best of my judgment; thus appealing from myself drunk to myself sober. I was engaged on *The Pleasures of Memory* for nine years; on *Human Life* for nearly the same space of time; and *Italy* occupied me little less than sixteen years.*

I was present when Sir Joshua Reynolds delivered his last lecture at the Royal Academy. On entering the room I found that a semicircle of chairs, immediately in front of the pulpit, was reserved for persons of distinction, being labelled " Mr. Burke," " Mr. Boswell," &c. &c.; and I, with other young men, was forced to station myself a good way off. During the lecture, a great crash was heard; and the company, fearing that the building was about to come down, rushed towards the door. Presently, however, it appeared that there was no cause for alarm;†

* I was with Mr. Rogers when he tore to pieces, and threw into the fire, a manuscript operatic drama, *The Vintage of Burgundy*, which he had written early in life. He told me that he offered it to a manager, who said, " I will bring it on the stage, if you are determined to have it acted; *but it will certainly be damned*."

† There *was* cause for alarm. " On an examination of the floor afterwards, it was found that one of the beams for its support had actually given way from the great weight of the assembly of persons who pressed upon it, and probably from a flaw also in the wood." Northcote's *Life of Reynolds*, ii. 263, ed. 1819.

and they endeavoured to resume their places; but, in consequence of the confusion, the reserved seats were now occupied by those who could first get into them; and I, pressing forward, secured one of them. Sir Joshua concluded the lecture by saying, with great emotion, " And I should desire that the last words which I should pronounce in this Academy and from this place might be the name of—Michael Angelo." As he descended from the rostrum, Burke went up to him, took his hand, and said,

> " The Angel ended, and in Adam's ear
> So charming left his voice, that he a while
> Thought him still speaking, still stood fix'd
> to hear."*

What a quantity of snuff Sir Joshua took! I once saw him at an Academy-dinner, when his waistcoat was absolutely powdered with it.

Sir Joshua was always thinking of his art. He was one day walking with Dr. Lawrence† near Beaconsfield, when they met a beautiful little peasant-boy. Sir Joshua, after looking earnestly at the child, exclaimed, " I must go home and deepen the colouring of my *Infant Hercules*." The boy was a good deal sun-burnt.

Count d'Adhemar was the original purchaser of Sir Joshua's *Muscipula*. Sir Joshua, who fancied that he was bargaining for a different and less important picture, told him that the

---

* *Par. Lost*, b. viii. 1.

† Dr. French Lawrence, M.P., the friend of Edmund Burke.—*Ed*.

price was fifty guineas; and on discovering the mistake, allowed him to have *Muscipula* for that sum.—Fox had been anxious to possess *Muscipula* when it was first painted; and he bought it at the Ambassador's sale for (I believe) fifty guineas. It is now at St. Anne's Hill. It would fetch, at the present day, a thousand guineas.

The morning of the day on which Sir Joshua's *Puck* was to be sold, Lord Farnborough and Dance the painter breakfasted with me; and we went to the sale together. When *Puck* was put up, it excited such admiration, that there was a general clapping of hands: yet it was knocked down to me at a comparatively trifling price.* I walked home from the sale, a man carrying *Puck* before me; and so well was the picture known, that more than one person, as they passed us in the street, called out, " There it is!"

I like Northcote's *Life of Sir Joshua:* it may be depended upon for facts; and, of course, Northcote was a very competent critic in painting.

I can hardly believe what was told me long

---

* " When the Shakespeare gallery was disposed of by lottery, the building itself, and many of the capital pictures, formed the principal prize, which was won by Mr. Tassie of Leicester Square, who, after showing it a few months, divided the property into several lots, and sold them by auction. In that sale the pictures of Sir Joshua produced the following sums, which are here contrasted with the prices paid to Sir Joshua by Mr. Boydell:

Prices paid to Sir Joshua by Mr. Boydell.	Prices for which they sold by auction.
* * *	* * * * *
Puck or Robin Good Fellow, 100 guineas.	£215 5s. 0d."

Edwards's *Anecdotes of Painters*, &c. p. 204.

ago by a gentleman living in the Temple, who, however, assured me that it was fact. He happened to be passing by Sir Joshua's house in Leicester Square, when he saw a poor girl seated on the steps and crying bitterly. He asked what was the matter; and she replied that she was crying, "because *the one shilling* which she had received from Sir Joshua for sitting to him as a model, had proved to be a bad one, and he would not give her another."

I recollect when it was still the fashion for gentlemen to wear swords. I have seen Haydn play at a concert in a tie-wig, with a sword at his side.

The head-dresses of the ladies, during my youth, were of a truly preposterous size. I have gone to Ranelagh in a coach with a lady who was obliged to sit upon a stool placed in the bottom of the coach, the height of her head-dress not allowing her to occupy the regular seat.

Their tight lacing was equally absurd. Lady Crewe told me, that, on returning home from Ranelagh, she has rushed up to her bed-room, and desired her maid to cut her laces without a moment's delay, for fear she should faint.

Doctor Fordyce sometimes drank a good deal at dinner. He was summoned one evening to see a lady patient, when he was more than half-seas-over, and conscious that he was so. Feeling her pulse, and finding himself unable to count its beats, he muttered, " Drunk, by God! " Next morning, recollecting the circumstance, he was greatly vexed: and just as he was thinking what explanation of his behaviour he should offer to the lady, a letter from her was put into his hand. " She too well knew," said the letter, " that he had discovered the unfortunate condition in which she was when he last visited her; and she entreated him to keep the matter secret in consideration of the enclosed (a hundred-pound bank-note)."

I have several times talked to a very aged boatman on the Thames, who recollected " Mr. Alexander Pope." This boatman, when a lad, had frequently assisted his father in rowing Pope up and down the river. On such occasions Pope generally sat in a sedan-chair.

When I first began to publish, I got acquainted with an elderly person named Lawless,* shopman of Messrs. Cadell and Davies the booksellers. Lawless told me, that he was once walking through Twickenham, accompanied by a friend, and a little boy the son of that friend. On the

* This Lawless (as I was informed by Mr. Maltby) used daily to eat his dinner in the shop, placing a large folio before him so as to conceal his plate. Often, to his great annoyance, just as he was beginning his meal, Gibbon would drop in, and ask a variety of questions about books. One day, Lawless, out of all patience at the interruption, exclaimed from behind the folio, " Mr. Gibbon, I'm at dinner, and can't answer any questions till I have finished it."

approach of a very diminutive, misshapen, and shabbily-dressed person, the child drew back half-afraid. " Don't be alarmed," said Lawless; " it is only a poor man."—" A poor man! " cried his friend: " why, that is Mr. Alexander Pope."

Lawless also told me that he had been intimate with the waiting-maid of Pope's beloved Martha Blount. According to the maid's account, her mistress was one of the best-natured and kindest persons possible: she would take her out in the carriage to see sights, &c. &c.

Long ago, when Pope's villa was for sale, I had a great wish to buy it; but I apprehended that it would fetch a much larger sum than it did; and moreover I dreaded the epigrams, &c., which would certainly have been levelled at me, if it had become mine.—The other day, when the villa was finally dismantled, I was anxious that the obelisk erected by Pope to his mother's memory should be placed in the gardens at Hampton Court, and I offered to contribute my mite for that purpose:—but, no!— and the obelisk is now at Gopsall, Lord Howe's seat in Leicestershire.

There are at Lord Bathurst's a good many unpublished letters of Pope, Bolingbroke, &c., which I have turned over. In one of them Bolingbroke says that he has no desire to " wrestle with a chimney-sweeper," that is, Warburton.—Lady Bathurst promised to send me some of Pope's letters: instead of which, she sent me a packet of letters from Queen Mary to King William, in which he is addressed as her " dear husb*an*."*

In Pope's noble lines *To the Earl of Oxford*, *prefixed to Parnell's Poems*, there is an impropriety which was forced upon the poet by the rhyme;

" The Muse attends thee to thy silent shade:

*   *   *   *   *   *   *

She waits, *or to the scaffold or the cell*,
When the last lingering friend has bid
    farewell."

It should be, of course, " or to the cell or the scaffold."

Pope has sometimes a beautiful line rhyming to a very indifferent one. For instance, in the *Epistle to Jervas*,

" Alas, how little from the grave we claim!
    Thou but preserv'st a face, and I a name: "

the latter line is very good: in the former, " claim " is forced and bad; it should have been " save " or " preserve." Again, in the *Elegy to the Memory of an Unfortunate Lady*,

* " Lord Bathurst has lent me a very entertaining collection of original letters, from Pope, Bolingbroke, Swift, Queen Mary, &c., and has promised to make me a present of any thing I like out of them. I cannot say these communications have given me a very great idea of Queen Mary's head; but her heart, I am persuaded, was a very good one. The defect must have been in her education; for such spelling and such English I never saw; romantic and childish too, as to sentiment. My reverence for her many virtues leads me to hope she was very young when she wrote them." Letter of Hannah More, in her *Memoirs*, &c. vol. i. 358, third ed.

" A heap of dust alone remains of thee;
    'Tis all thou art, and all the proud shall be,"

the former line is touching, the latter bad.

What a charming line is that in *The Rape of the Lock!*

" If to her share some female errors fall,
    Look on her face, and you'll forget them all."

These verses in his *Imitation of the Second Epistle of the Second Book of Horace* (verses which Lord Holland is so fond of hearing me repeat) are as good as any in Horace himself;

" Years following years, steal something every
    day,
    At last they steal us from ourselves away;
    In one our frolics, one amusements end,
    In one a mistress drops, in one a friend."

But perhaps the best line Pope ever wrote is in his *Imitation of the First Satire of the Second Book of Horace;*

" Bare the mean heart that lurks beneath a
    star."

The want of pauses is the main blemish in Pope's versification: I can't recollect at this moment any pause he has, except that in his *Prologue to Cato;*

16

" *The triumph ceas'd;* tears gush'd from every
    eye;
  The world's great victor pass'd unheeded by."

People are now so fond of *the obscure* in poetry,
that they can perceive no *deep thinking* in that
darling man Pope, because he always expresses
himself with such admirable clearness.

My father used to recommend Pope's *Homer* to
me: but, with all my love of Pope, I never could
like it. (I delight in Cowper's *Homer;* I have
read it again and again.)

Pope is not to be compared to Dryden for
varied harmony of versification; nor for ease;—
how naturally the words follow each other in
this couplet of Dryden's in the *Second Part of
Absalom and Achitophel!*

" The midwife laid her hand on his thick skull,
  With this prophetic blessing—*Be thou dull!* "

and in that touching one in his *Epistle to Congreve,*

" Be kind to my remains; and, O, defend,
  Against your judgment, your departed
    friend! "

Dryden's *Virgil* is, on the whole, a failure; but
I am not sure that it does not exhibit the best
specimens of his versification: in that work he
had not to tax his invention; he had only to

think of the expression and versification. It contains one thing, in the supplication of Turnus to Æneas, which is finer than the original;

> " Yet think, O, think, if mercy may be shown,—
> Thou hadst a father once, *and hast a son*,—
> Pity my sire," &c.

Virgil's words are:

> " Miseri te si qua parentis
> Tangere cura potest, oro,—fuit et tibi talis
> Anchises genitor,—Dauni miserere senectæ,"
> &c.*

I sometimes wonder† how a man can ever be cheerful, when he knows that he *must* die. But what poets write about *the horrors of the grave* makes not the slightest impression upon me; for instance, what Dryden says;

> " Vain men! how vanishing a bliss we crave!
> Now warm in love, now withering in the
>   grave!
> Never, O, never more, to see the sun,
> Still dark, in a damp vault, and still alone! "‡

* *Æn.* xii. 932.

† Mr. Rogers once made the same remark to Mr. Luttrell (*see* note, p. 227), who versified it as follows;
> " O death, thy certainty is such,
>   And thou'rt a thing so fearful,
> That, musing, I have wonder'd much
>   How men were ever cheerful."

‡ *Palamon and Arcite*, b. iii.

18

All this is unphilosophical; in fact, nonsense. The body, when the soul has left it, is as worthless as an old garment,—rather more so, for it rots much sooner.—The lines of Dryden which I have just quoted (and which are modernised from Chaucer) were great favourites with Sheridan; I seem now to hear him reciting them.

Quin (as Sir George Beaumont told me) was once at a very small dinner-party. The master of the house, pushing a delicious pudding towards Quin, begged him to taste it. A gentleman had just before helped himself to an immense piece of it. " Pray," said Quin, looking first at the gentleman's plate and then at the dish, " which *is* the pudding? "

Sir George Beaumont, when a young man, was one day in the Mount (a famous coffee-house in Mount Street, Grosvenor Square) with Harvey Aston. Various persons were seated at different tables. Among others present, there was an Irishman who was very celebrated as a duellist, having killed at least half-a-dozen antagonists. Aston, talking to some of his acquaintance, swore that he would make the duellist stand barefooted before them. " You had better take care what you say," they replied; " he has his eye upon you."—" No matter," rejoined Aston; " I declare again that he shall stand barefooted before you, if you will make up among you a purse of fifty guineas." They did so. Aston then said in a loud voice, " I have been in Ireland, and am well acquainted with the natives." The Irishman was all ear. Aston went on, " The Irish, being born in bogs, are every one of them web-footed; I know it for a fact."—" Sir," roared the duellist, starting up from his table, " it is false! " Aston persisted in his assertion. " Sir," cried the other, " *I* was born in Ireland; and I will prove to you that it is a falsehood." So saying, in great haste he pulled off his shoes and stockings, and displayed his bare feet. The joke ended in Aston's sharing the purse between the Irishman and himself, giving the former thirty guineas, and keeping twenty. Sir George assured me that this was a true story.*

Aston was always making disturbances. I remember being at Ranelagh with my father and mother, when we heard a great uproar, and were told that it was occasioned by Aston.

If I mistake not, Aston fought two duels in India on two successive days, and fell in the second one.†

* A similar story is related of the Irishman from whom Macklin took the idea of Sir Callaghan O'Brallaghan (in *Love à la Mode*). Macklin professing his belief that he, like other Irishmen, must have a tail, " he instantly pulled off his coat and waistcoat, to convince him of his mistake, assuring him, ' that no Irishman, *in that respect,* was better than another man.' " Cooke's *Memoirs of Macklin*, p. 225.

† " 1798, Dec. 23. At Madras, in consequence of a wound he received in a duel with Major Allen, of which he languished about a week, Col. Harvey Aston. He had been engaged in a similar affair of honour, and on the same account, with Major Picton, only the day preceding that on which he met Major A., but which was fortunately terminated by each party firing in the air, and a proper explanation taking place as to the offence." *Gentleman's Magazine,* vol. lxix. P. I. p. 527.—Aston had fought a duel in 1790 with Lieut. Fitzgerald, and was severely wounded. See Haydn's *Dict. of Dates,* sub *Duelling.*

That beautiful view of Conway Castle [in Mr. Rogers's dining-room] was painted by Sir George Beaumont, who presented it to me as a memorial of our having been originally introduced to each other in its ruins.—Sir George and I were always excellent friends. The morning after I arrived at Venice (on my first visit to Italy), I was looking out at the window, when I saw a gentleman and a lady land at my lodging from a gondola: they were Sir George and Lady Beaumont. The meeting was delightful:—even now, I think of it with pleasure.

In my youthful days Young's *Night-Thoughts* was a very favourite book, especially with ladies: I knew more than one lady who had a copy of it in which particular passages were marked for her by some popular preacher.

Young's poem *The Last Day* contains, amidst much absurdity, several very fine lines: what an *enormous* thought is this!—

" Those overwhelming armies, whose command
    Said to one empire ' Fall,' another ' Stand,'
    Whose rear lay rapt in night, while breaking dawn
    Rous'd the broad front, and call'd the battle on."*

At Brighton, during my youth, I became acquainted with a lawyer who had known Gray. He said that Gray's pronunciation was very affected, *e.g.* " What *naise* (noise) is that? "

* Book ii.

Henley (the translator of Beckford's *Vathek*) was one morning paying a visit to Gray, when a dog came into the room. " Is that your dog? " said Henley. " No," replied Gray: " do you suppose that *I* would keep an animal *by which I might possibly lose my life?* "

I was a mere lad when Mason's *Gray* was published. I read it in my young days with delight, and have done so ever since: the Letters have for me an inexpressible charm; they are as witty as Walpole's, and have, what his want, true wisdom. I used to take a pocket edition of Gray's *Poems* with me during my morning walks to town to my father's banking-house, where I was a clerk, and read them by the way. I can repeat them all.

I *do* envy Gray these lines in his *Ode on a distant prospect of Eton College;*

" Still as they run, they look behind,
    They hear a voice in every wind,
            And snatch a fearful joy."

But what immediately follows is not good;

" Gay Hope is theirs, by Fancy fed,
            Less pleasing *when possess'd:* "

we cannot be said to *possess* hope.—How strange it is that, with all Gray's care in composition, the word " shade " should occur three times in the course of the eleven first lines of that ode!—

" Her Henry's holy *shade*."
" Whose turf, whose *shade*, whose flowers
    among."
" Ah happy hills, ah pleasing *shade!* "

Both Fox and Courtenay thought Gray's
fragment, *The Alliance of Education and Government*,
his finest poem: but that was because they
preferred the heroic couplet to every other kind
of verse. A celebrated passage in it,—

> " Oft o'er the trembling nations from afar
> Has Scythia breathed the living cloud of war;
> And, where the deluge burst with sweepy
>   sway,
> Their arms, their kings, their gods were roll'd
>   away.
> As oft have issu'd, host impelling host,
> The blue-ey'd myriads from the Baltic coast:
> The prostrate south to the destroyer yields
> Her boasted titles and her golden fields;
> With grim delight the brood of winter view
> A brighter day and heavens of azure hue,
> Scent the new fragrance of the breathing rose,
> And quaff the *pendent vintage* as it grows,"—

is a good deal injured by the forced and
unnatural expression, " pendent vintage."*
    I once read Gray's *Ode to Adversity* to Words-
worth; and at the line,—

---

* For this expression Gray was indebted to Virgil:
       " Non eadem arboribus *pendet vindemia* nostris
       Quam Methymnæo carpit de palmite Lesbos."
                        Georg. ii. 89.

" And leave us leisure to be good,"—

Wordsworth exclaimed, " I am quite sure *that* is not original; Gray could not have hit upon it."*

The stanza which Gray threw out of his *Elegy* is better than some of the stanzas he has retained;

" There scatter'd oft, the earliest of the year,
 By hands unseen, are showers of violets found;
The redbreast loves to build and warble there,
 And little footsteps lightly print the ground."

I believe few people know, what I have been told as fact, that the *Macleane* who was hanged for robbery, and is mentioned in Gray's *Long Story*,—

" He stood as mute as poor *Macleane*,"—

was brother to *Maclaine*, the translator of Mosheim.

I think it is Gray who somewhere says that monosyllables should be avoided in poetry: but there are many lines consisting only of monosyllables, which could not possibly be improved. For instance, in Shakespeare's *Romeo and Juliet*,—

" Thou canst not speak of what thou dost not feel;"

* The Rev. J. Mitford, in his ed. of Gray, cites ad l.,
 " And know, I have not yet *the leisure to be good*."
   Oldham, *Ode*, st. 5,—*Works*, i. 85, ed. 1722.

and in Pope's *Eloisa to Abelard,*—

> " Pant on thy lip, and to thy heart be prest;
>   Give all thou canst, and let me dream the
>   rest."

Matthias* showed me the papers belonging to Pembroke Hall, Cambridge, which he had borrowed for his edition of *Gray*; and among them were several very indecent poems by Gray's friend West, in whose day it was the fashion for young men to write in that style.   If West had lived, he would have been no mean poet: he has left some lines which are certainly among the happiest imitations of Pope;

> " How weak is man to reason's judging eye!
>   Born in this moment, in the next we die;
>   Part mortal clay, and part ethereal fire,
>   Too proud to creep, too humble to aspire."

When I was at Nuneham, I read Mason's manuscript letters to Lord Harcourt, which contain nothing to render them worth printing. They evince the excessive deference which Mason showed to Gray,—" Mr. Gray's opinion " being frequently quoted.   There is in them a very gross passage about Lady M. W. Montagu.

Mason's poetry is, on the whole, stiff and tiresome.   His best line is in the *Elegy on Lady Coventry;*

---

* T. J. Matthias, author of *The Pursuits of Literature*, 1794–6–7.—Ed.

" Yes, Coventry is dead.   Attend the strain,
   Daughters of Albion! ye that, light as air,
So oft have tripp'd in her fantastic train,
   With hearts as gay, and faces half as fair."

Topham Beauclerk (Johnson's friend) was a strangely absent person.   One day he had a party coming to dinner; and, just before their arrival, he went upstairs to change his dress. He forgot all about them; thought that it was bed-time, pulled off his clothes, and got into bed. A servant, who presently entered the room to tell him that his guests were waiting for him, found him fast asleep.

I remember taking Beattie's *Minstrel* down from my father's shelves, on a fine summer evening, and reading it, for the first time, with such delight!   It still charms me (I mean the First Book; the Second Book is very inferior).

During my youth umbrellas were far from common.   At that time every gentleman's family had *one umbrella,*—a huge thing, made of coarse cotton,—which used to be taken out with the carriage, and which, if there was rain, the footman held over the ladies' heads, as they entered, or alighted from, the carriage.

My first visit to France was in company with

Boddington,* not long before the Revolution began.   When we arrived at Calais, we saw both ladies and gentlemen walking on the pier with small fox-muffs.   While we were dining there, a poor monk came into the room and asked us for charity; and B. annoyed me much by saying to him, " Il faut travailler."†   The monk bowed meekly, and withdrew.   Nothing would satisfy B. but that we should ride on horseback the first stage from Calais; and accordingly, to the great amusement of the inn-keeper and chamber-maid, we were furnished with immense jack-boots and hoisted upon our steeds.   When we reached Paris, Lafayette gave us a general invitation to dine with him every day.   At his table we once dined with about a dozen persons (among them the Duke de la Rochefoucauld, Condorcet, &c.), most of whom afterwards came to an untimely end.

At a dinner-party in Paris, given by a French nobleman, I saw a black bottle of English porter set on the table as a great rarity, and drunk out of small glasses.

Boddington had a wretchedly bad memory;

* Samuel Boddington, later partner to Richard Sharp. His only child married the second son of Lady Holland by her first husband, Sir Godfrey Webster, from whom she was divorced by Act of Parliament.—*Ed.*

† " But we distinguish, said I, laying my hand upon the sleeve of his [the Monk's] tunic, in return for his appeal,—we distinguish, my good father, betwixt *those who wish only to eat the bread of their own labour*, and those who eat the bread of other people's, and have no other plan in life but to get through it in sloth and ignorance, *for the love of God.*"   Sterne's *Sentimental Journey,—The Monk.*

and, in order to improve it, he attended Feinaigle's lectures on the Art of Memory. Soon after, somebody asked Boddington the name of the lecturer; and, for his life, he could not recollect it.—When I was asked if I had attended the said lectures on the Art of Memory, I replied, " No: I wished to learn the Art of Forgetting."

One morning, when I was a lad, Wilkes came into our banking-house to solicit my father's vote. My father happened to be out; and I, as his representative, spoke to Wilkes. At parting, Wilkes shook hands with me; and I felt proud of it for a week after.

He was quite as ugly, and squinted as much, as his portraits make him; but he was very gentle-manly in appearance and manners. I think I see him at this moment, walking through the crowded streets of the city, as Chamberlain, on his way to Guildhall, in a scarlet coat, military boots, and a bag-wig,—the hackney-coachmen in vain calling out to him, " A coach, your honour? "

Words are so twisted and tortured by some writers of the present day, that I am really sorry for them,—I mean, for the words. It is a favourite fancy of mine that perhaps in the next world the use of words may be dispensed with,— that our thoughts may stream into each others' minds without any verbal communication.

When a young man, I went to Edinburgh,
carrying letters of introduction (from Dr. Kippis,
Dr. Price, &c.) to Adam Smith, Robertson, and
others. When I first saw Smith, he was at
breakfast, eating strawberries; and he descanted
on the superior flavour of those grown in Scotland.
I found him very kind and communicative. He
was (what Robertson was not) a man who had
seen a great deal of the world. Once, in the
course of conversation, I happened to remark of
some writer, that " he was rather superficial,—
a Voltaire."—" Sir," cried Smith, striking the
table with his hand, " there has been but *one*
Voltaire! "

Robertson, too, was very kind to me. He,
one morning, spread out the map of Scotland on
the floor, and got upon his knees, to describe
the route I ought to follow in making a tour on
horseback through the Highlands.

At Edinburgh I became acquainted with
Henry Mackenzie, who asked me to correspond
with him; which I (then young, romantic, and
an admirer of his *Julia de Roubignè*) willingly
agreed to. We accordingly wrote to each other
occasionally during several years; but his letters,
to my surprise and disappointment, were of the
most commonplace description. Yet his published writings display no ordinary talent; and,
like those of Beattie, they are remarkable for a
pure English idiom,—which cannot be said of
Hume's writings, beautiful as *they* are.

The most memorable day perhaps which I
ever passed was at Edinburgh,—a Sunday;

when, after breakfasting with Robertson, I heard him preach in the forenoon, and Blair in the afternoon, then took coffee with the Piozzis, and supped with Adam Smith. Robertson's sermon was excellent both for matter and manner of delivery. Blair's was good, but less impressive; and his broad Scotch accent offended my ears greatly.

My acquaintance with Mr. and Mrs. Piozzi began at Edinburgh, being brought about by the landlord of the hotel where they and I were staying. He thought that I should be gratified by " hearing Mr. Piozzi's piano-forte: " and they called upon me, on learning from the landlord who I was, and that Adam Smith, Robertson, and Mackenzie had left cards for me.

I was afterwards very intimate with the Piozzis, and visited them often at Streatham. The world was most unjust in blaming Mrs. Thrale for marrying Piozzi: he was a very handsome, gentlemanly, and amiable person, and made her a very good husband. In the evening he used to play to us most beautifully on the piano. Her daughters never would see her after that marriage; and (poor woman) when she was at a very great age, I have heard her say that " she would go down upon her knees to them, if they would only be reconciled to her."*

* In *The Times* for Feb. 20th, 1856, I am charged by a Mr. Hamilton Gray with misrepresenting (or rather with inventing) this passage. " I had," he says, " the pleasure of the acquaintance of the late Mr. Rogers, and, as I believe he was in the habit of speaking truth, I am convinced that his ' table-talk ' never did comprise such

(*continued on next page*)

I never saw Burns: I was within thirty miles of Dumfries when he was living there; and yet I did not go to visit him; which I have regretted ever since.—I think his *Cottar's Saturday-Night* the finest pastoral in any language.

How incapable of estimating Burns's genius were the worthy folks of Edinburgh! Henry Mackenzie (who ought to have known better) advised him to take for his model in song-writing—Mrs. John Hunter!*

(continued from previous page)
mis-statements as the above. . . . . After the return of Mr. and Mrs. Piozzi from the protracted tour which they made after their marriage on the Continent, Viscountess Keith, then Miss Thrale, and her sisters were on a footing of frequent intercourse with Mr. and Mrs. Piozzi. They received them at their house, and visited them; and this amicable intercourse continued until Mrs. Piozzi's death, at an advanced age." Now, I most positively assert that Mr. Rogers used the very words in question; and I am much mistaken if several gentlemen who, like myself, were constant visitors at St. James's Place, would not at once confirm my assertion. That his memory sometimes deceived him, is not to be denied; and such, it appears, was the case when he stated that all intercourse had ceased between Mrs. Piozzi and her daughters: but I have so often heard him repeat Mrs. Piozzi's declaration that " she would go down upon her knees to them, if they would only be reconciled to her," that, in spite of what is stated by Mr. Hamilton Gray, I believe that Mrs. Piozzi on some occasion *did* complain to Mr. Rogers of the alienation of her family. Let me add, that the present volume contains throughout such evidence of my anxiety to record the conversation of Mr. Rogers with correctness, as ought to have saved me from the impertinence of Mr. Hamilton Gray.

* On this passage an accomplished northern critic (Mr. Carruthers) has remarked; " Mr. Rogers was in error here. Henry Mackenzie from the first hailed Burns as a genius of no ordinary rank, irrespective of his humble condition in society. It was Dr. Gregory who recommended the poems of Mrs. Hunter to Burns, not as his model in song-writing, but to show how much correctness and high polish enhance the value of short occasional poems." *The Inverness Courier* for Feb. 14, 1856.—As a writer of songs, Mrs. Hunter is, no doubt, immeasurably inferior to Burns: but her Cherokee *Death-Song*, and several other small pieces which she wrote for music, are far from contemptible: see her *Poems*, 1802.

Sir John Henry Moore, who died in his twenty-fourth year, possessed considerable talent. His *L'Amour timide* is very pretty.

[" *L'Amour timide.*
If in that breast, so good, so pure,
    Compassion ever lov'd to dwell,
Pity the sorrows I endure;
    The cause—I must not, dare not tell.

The grief that on my quiet preys—*
    That rends my heart—that checks my
        tongue,—
I fear will last me all my days,
    But feel it will not last me long."]

Marivaux's† *Marianne* is a particular favourite with me: I have read it six times through; and I have shed tears over it, after I was seventy,—not so much at its pathos as at its generous sentiments.

The Abbé Delille (whom I knew well and liked much) was of opinion that Marivaux's *Paysan Parvenu* was a greater literary effort than *Marianne*.

* Mr. Rogers, I believe, was not aware that the second stanza is taken from Montreuil;
    " Ne me demandez plus, Sylvie,
      Quel est le mal que je ressens.
    C'est un mal que j'auray tout le temps de ma vie,
      Mais je ne l'auray pas long-temps."
                    Œuvres, p. 602, ed. 1666.
† Mr. Rogers's admiration of this writer induced him to purchase his picture at the Strawberry-Hill sale;—a miniature, by Liotard, which had been painted for Horace Walpole.

I once said to Delille, " Don't you think that Voltaire's *vers de société* are the first of their kind? " He replied, " Assuredly; the very first, and—the last."

Dr. Parr had a great deal of sensibility. When I read to him, in Lincoln's Inn Fields, the account of O'Coigly's* death, the tears rolled down his cheeks.

One day, Mackintosh having vexed him by calling O'Coigly " a rascal," Parr immediately rejoined, " Yes, Jamie, he was a bad man, but he might have been worse; he was an Irishman, but he might have been a Scotchman; he was a priest, but he might have been a lawyer; he was a republican, but he might have been an apostate."

After their quarrel (about Gerald)†, Parr often spoke with much bitterness of Mackintosh: among other severe things, he said that " Mackintosh came up from Scotland with a metaphysical head, a cold heart, and open hands." At last they were reconciled, having met, for that purpose, in my house: but their old familiarity was never fully re-established.

Parr was frequently very tiresome in conversation, talking like a schoolmaster.

* James O'Coigly (alias James Quigley, alias James John Fivey) was tried for high treason at Maidstone, and hanged on Penningdon Heath, 7th June, 1798. When he had hung about ten minutes, he was beheaded; and the head and body were immediately buried under the gallows (the rest of his sentence,—that, " while he was yet alive, his bowels should be taken out and burnt before his face," &c., having been remitted).

† Joseph Gerrald (1763–96), political reformer and Parr's pupil, transported in 1794.

He had a horror of the east wind; and Tom Sheridan once kept him prisoner in the house for a fortnight by fixing the weathercock in that direction.

We have not a few charming prose-writers in what may be called the middle style,—Addison, Middleton, Jortin, &c.; but in the highest prose-style we have none to be compared with Bossuet, Pascal, or Buffon.—We have far better tragic writers than Corneille or Racine; but we have no one to be compared with Moliere,— no one *like* him.

Swift's verses on his own death have an exquisite facility: but we are not to suppose that he wrote them off-hand; their ease is the result of very careful composition.

Helen Maria Williams* was a very fascinating person; but not handsome. I knew her intimately in her youth, when she resided in London with her mother and sisters. They used to give very agreeable evening-parties, at which I have met many of the Scotch literati, Lord Monboddo, &c.

Late in life, Helen translated into English, and very beautiful English too, Humboldt's long work, *Personal Narrative of Travels*, &c.; and, I

* Poetess; protégée of Anna Seward; and ardent supporter of the French Revolution.—*Ed.*

believe, nearly the whole impression still lies in Longman's warehouse.

When she was in Paris, during the Revolution, she has seen men and women, who were waiting for admission at the door of the theatre, suddenly leave their station on the passing of a set of wretches going to be guillotined, and then, after having ascertained that none of their relations or friends were among them, very unconcernedly return to the door of the theatre.—I have frequently dined with her at Paris, when Kosciusko and other celebrated persons were of the party.

When Lord Erskine heard that somebody had died worth two hundred thousand pounds, he observed, " Well, that's a very pretty sum to begin the next world with."

" A friend of mine," said Erskine, " was suffering from a continual wakefulness; and various methods were tried to send him to sleep, but in vain. At last his physicians resorted to an experiment which succeeded perfectly: they dressed him in a watchman's coat, put a lantern into his hand, placed him in a sentry-box, and— he was asleep in ten minutes."

To all letters soliciting his " subscription " to any thing, Erskine had a regular form of reply, viz. " Sir, I feel much honoured by your application to me, and I beg to subscribe " —here the reader had to turn over the leaf— " myself your very ob^t servant," &c.

35

I wish I could recollect all the anecdotes of his early life which Erskine used to relate with such spirit and dramatic effect. He had been in the navy; and he said that he once managed to run a vessel between two rocks, where it seemed almost impossible that she could have been driven. He had also been in the army; and on one occasion saved the life of a soldier who was condemned to death, by making an earnest appeal in his behalf to the general in command and his wife: Erskine having got the pardon, rode off with it at full speed to the place of execution, where he arrived just as the soldier was kneeling, and the muskets were levelled for the fatal shot.

Erskine used to say that when the hour came that all secrets should be revealed, we should know the reason why—shoes are always made too tight.

When he had a house at Hampstead, he entertained the very best company. I have dined there with the Prince of Wales,—the only time I ever had any conversation with his royal highness. On that occasion the Prince was very agreeable and familiar. Among other anecdotes which he told us of Lord Thurlow, I remember these two. The first was: Thurlow once said to the Prince, " Sir, your father will continue to be a popular king as long as he continues to go to church every Sunday, and to be faithful to that ugly woman, your mother; but you, sir, will never be popular." The other was this: While his servants were carrying

Thurlow up stairs to his bed-room, just before his death, they happened to let his legs strike against the banisters, upon which he uttered *the last words he ever spoke,*—a frightful imprecation on " all their souls."

Erskine said that the Prince of Wales was quite " a cosmogony man " (alluding to *The Vicar of Wakefield*), for he had only two classical quotations,—one from Homer and one from Virgil,—which he never failed to sport when there was any opportunity of introducing them.

Latterly Erskine was very poor; and no wonder, for he always contrived to sell out of the funds when they were very low, and to buy in when they were very high. " By heaven," he would say, " I am a perfect kite, all paper; the boys might fly me." Yet, poor as he was, he still kept the best society: I have met him at the Duke of York's, &c. &c.

Here's an epigram by Erskine which is far from bad (I know not if it has ever been printed);

" The French have taste in all they do,
    Which we are quite without;
For Nature, that to them gave *goût,*
    To us gave only gout."

Thomas Grenville told me this curious fact. When he was a young man, he one day dined with Lord Spencer at Wimbledon. Among the company was George Pitt (afterwards Lord Rivers), who declared that he could tame the most furious animal by looking at it steadily. Lord Spencer said, " Well, there is a mastiff in the court-yard here, which is the terror of the neighbourhood: will you try your powers on him? " Pitt agreed to do so; and the company descended into the court-yard. A servant held the mastiff by a chain. Pitt knelt down at a short distance from the animal, and stared him sternly in the face. They all shuddered. At a signal given, the mastiff was let loose, and rushed furiously towards Pitt,—then suddenly checked his pace, seemed confounded, and, leaping over Pitt's head, ran away, and was not seen for many hours after.

During one of my visits to Italy, while I was walking, a little before my carriage, on the road, not far from Vicenza, I perceived two huge dogs, nearly as tall as myself, bounding towards me (from out a gateway, though there was no house in sight). I recollected what Pitt had done; and trembling from head to foot, I yet had resolution enough to stand quite still and eye them with a fixed look. They gradually relaxed their speed from a gallop to a trot, came up to me, stopped for a moment, and then went back again.

Dunning (afterwards Lord Ashburton) was " stating the law " to a jury at Guildhall, when Lord Mansfield interrupted him by saying, " If *that* be law, I'll go home and burn my books." —" My Lord," replied Dunning, " you had better go home and *read* them."

Dunning was remarkably ugly. One night, while he was playing whist, at Nando's, with Horne Tooke and two others, Lord Thurlow called at the door, and desired the waiter to give a note to Dunning (with whom, though their politics were so different, he was very intimate). The waiter did not know Dunning by sight. " Take the note up stairs," said Thurlow, " and deliver it to the ugliest man at the card-table— to him who most resembles the knave of spades." The note immediately reached its destination.— Horne Tooke used often to tell this anecdote.

When I was young, we had (what we have not now) several country-gentlemen of considerable literary celebrity,—for instance, Hayley, Sargent (author of *The Mine*), and Webb. There are some good remarks on painting and on poetry scattered through Webb's different pieces.

If Hayley was formerly over-rated, he is now undervalued. He was a most accomplished person, as indeed is evident from the notes to his various poems,—notes which Lord Holland admires greatly.* His translation of the First Canto of the *Inferno*† is on the whole good; but he has omitted some of the striking circumstances in the original.

* " Lord Holland, the best-informed and most elegant of our writers on the subject of the Spanish theatre, declared that he had been induced to learn that language by what Hayley had written concerning the poet Ercilla." Cary's *Life of Hayley,—Lives of English Poets*, &c. p. 347.

† In the Notes to his *Essay on Epic Poetry*.

When I first came forward as a poet, I was highly gratified by the praise which Hayley bestowed on my writings, and which was communicated to me by Cadell the publisher.

I once travelled with Lord Lansdowne (when Lord Henry Petty) to Bognor, in the neighbourhood of which Hayley was then living (not at Eartham, but in a village* near it). I went to visit him. The door was opened by a little girl; and when I said, " Is Mr. Hayley at home? " he himself exclaimed, " Yes, he is "— (he recognised my voice, though we had only met once before,—at Flaxman's); and out he came, adding, " I am delighted to see you: if I had not known your voice, I should not have let you in, for I am very busy." I took coffee with him, and he talked most agreeably. I said that Lord Henry Petty was my travelling companion, and that he was very anxious to be introduced to him: but Hayley, who did not care a straw for rank, could not be prevailed upon to see his lordship.

In those days, indeed, praise was sweet to me, even when it came from those who were far inferior to Hayley: what pleasure I felt on being told that Este had said of me, " A child of Goldsmith, sir! "

Parson Este, in conjunction with Captain Topham, edited the newspaper called *The World*.† He was reader at Whitehall; and he read the

* Felpham.
† The organ of the Della Cruscan cult.—*Ed*.

service so admirably, that Mrs. Siddons used frequently to go to hear him. My sister and I once took him with us on a little tour; and when we were at Ross, he read to us Pope's lines about "the man of Ross,"—I cannot describe how beautifully.

Este published a strange book, *My own Life*, and *A Journey through Flanders*, &c. He used to throw himself into attitudes in the street. At last he went mad, and died insane.

I wish somebody would collect all the Epigrams written by Dr. Mansel (Master of Trinity College, Cambridge, and Bishop of Bristol): they are remarkably neat and clever.

When titled ladies become authoresses or composers, their friends suffer for it. Lady —— asked me to buy her book; and I replied that I would do so when I was rich enough. I went to a concert at Lady ——'s, during which several pieces composed by her daughter were performed; and early next morning, a music-seller arrived at my house, bringing with him the daughter's compositions (and a bill receipted), price sixteen shillings.

Surely, in delicate touches of pathos Homer excels all poets. For instance, how beautiful is Andromache's saying, after Hector's death, that

Astyanax had lost *his playfellow;* and Helen's declaration concerning the same hero, that *he* had never reproached her!

[" Thee lost, he loses all, of father, both,
    And equal playmate in one day depriv'd."
                Cowper's *Iliad*, b. xxii.

 " Yet never heard I once hard speech from thee
    Or taunt morose; but if it ever chanc'd
    That male or female of thy father's house
    Blam'd me, and even if herself the queen
    (For in the king, whate'er befell, I found
    Always a father), thou hast interpos'd
    Thy gentle temper and thy gentle speech
    To soothe them."   *Id*. b. xxiv.]

John Hunter* believed that when there was only one daughter and several sons in a family, the daughter was always of a masculine disposition; and that when a family consisted of several daughters and only one son, the son was always effeminate. Payne Knight used to say that Homer seems to have entertained the same idea; for in the *Iliad* we find that Dolon, who proves to be such a coward, was an only son and had several sisters.

[" There was one Dolon in the camp of Troy,
    Son of Eumedes, herald of the gods,
    Who with five daughters had no son beside."
                Cowper's *Iliad*, b. x.]

* The surgeon.—*Ed*.

Some traveller relates, that an Indian being asleep in his canoe, which was fastened to the shore, a little above the Falls of Niagara, an English soldier wantonly cut the fastenings, and the canoe drifted into the current;—that the Indian, after vainly trying the use of his paddles, and perceiving that he was just approaching the Falls, covered his head with his mat, lay down in the canoe, and calmly resigned himself to his fate. So Homer, following nature, tells us in the *Odyssey* that Ulysses, when his companions had opened the bag which contained the winds, covered his head with his mantle, and lay down in the vessel.

["They loos'd the bag; forth issu'd all the winds,
And, rapt by tempests back, with fruitless tears
They mourn'd their native country lost again.
Just then awaking, in my troubled mind
I doubted, whether from the vessel's side
To plunge and perish, or with patient mind
To suffer and to live.   The sufferer's part
At length I chose, and resolute surviv'd.
But, with my mantle wrapp'd around my brows,
I laid me down, till, hurried by the blast,
We, groaning, reach'd again th' Æolian isle."

Cowper's *Odyssey*, b. x.]

It is inexcusable in any one to write illegibly. When I was a schoolboy, I used to get hold of our writing-master's copies and trace them by holding them against the window: hence the plain hand I now write.—When the great Lord Clive was in India, his sisters sent him some handsome presents from England; and he informed them by letter that he had returned them an " *elephant* " (at least so they read the word); an announcement which threw them into the utmost perplexity,—for what could they possibly do with the animal? The true word was " equivalent."*

Romney the painter used to say that the Grecian architecture was the invention of glorious men, but the Gothic that of gods.

Thomas Grenville told me that he was present in the House when Lord North, suddenly rising from his seat and going out, carried off on the hilt of his sword the wig of Welbore Ellis, who was stooping to take up some papers. —I have myself often seen Lord North in the House. While sitting there, he would frequently

* Those who have seen autograph letters of Dr. Parr will not easily believe that any handwriting could be more puzzling. A Fellow of Magdalen College (who himself told me the circumstance) received one day a note from Parr, to say that he was on his way to Oxford, would sup with him that night, and would be glad to have *two eggs* (so my informant read the words) got ready for his supper. Accordingly, on his arrival, the eggs were served up in all due form to the hungry Doctor, who no sooner saw them than he flew into a violent passion. Instead of *eggs* he had written *lobsters*.

hold a handkerchief to his face; and once, after a long debate, when somebody said to him, " My lord, I fear you have been asleep," he replied, " I wish I had."

Sheridan, Tickell, and the rest of their set delighted in all sorts of practical jokes. For instance, while they were staying with Mr. and Mrs. Crewe (at Crewe Hall), Mrs. Sheridan and Mrs. Crewe would be driving out in the carriage, Sheridan and Tickell* riding on before them: suddenly, the ladies would see Sheridan stretched upon the ground, apparently in the agonies of death, and Tickell standing over him in a theatrical attitude of despair.—Again, Mr. Crewe expressed a great desire to meet Richardson (author of *The Fugitive*), of whom he had heard Sheridan and Tickell talk with much admiration. " I have invited him here," said Sheridan, " and he will positively be with us to-morrow." Next day, accordingly, Richardson made his appearance, and horrified the Crewes by the vulgarity and oddness of his manners and language. The fact was, Sheridan had got one of Mr. Crewe's tenants to personate Richardson for the occasion.—I don't know whether Richardson's *Fugitive* is a good comedy or not: but I know that Mrs. Jordan played very sweetly in it, and that Wewitzer performed a Frenchman most amusingly.

* Is it necessary to mention that Tickell (author of *The Wreath of Fashion*, a poem, of *Anticipation*, a prose pamphlet, &c. &c.) was one of Sheridan's most intimate friends; and that he and Sheridan had married sisters ?

I'll tell you another of Sheridan's youthful pranks. One night, as he, Fitzpatrick, and Lord John Townshend, came out of Drury-lane Theatre, they observed, among the vehicles in waiting, a very handsome phaeton with a groom in it. Sheridan asked the groom to let him get into the phaeton for five minutes, just to try it. The man consented, and stepped down. Sheridan got in, made Fitzpatrick and Townshend get in also, and then drove off at full speed for Vauxhall, whither they were pursued by the groom and a great crowd, shouting and halooing after them. At Vauxhall the groom recovered the phaeton, and was pacified by the present of a few shillings. But it would seem that this exploit had been attended with some unpleasant consequences to Sheridan, for he could not bear any allusion to it: he would say, " Pray, do not mention such an absurd frolic."

I was present on the second day of Hastings's trial in Westminster Hall; when Sheridan was listened to with such attention that you might have heard a pin drop.—During one of those days Sheridan, having observed Gibbon among the audience, took occasion to mention " the luminous author of *The Decline and Fall*."*

* But, as reported in *The Morning Chronicle*, June 14, 1788, the expression used by Sheridan was " the correct periods of Tacitus or the *luminous page of Gibbon*."—" Before my departure from England, I was present at the august spectacle of Mr. Hastings's trial in Westminster Hall. It is not my province to absolve or condemn the Governor of India; but Mr. Sheridan's eloquence demanded my applause; nor could I hear without emotion the personal compliment which he paid me in the presence of the British nation."—Gibbon's *Memoirs*, &c. p. 172, ed. 4to.

After he had finished, one of his friends reproached him with flattering Gibbon. " Why, what did I say of him? " asked Sheridan.—" You called him the luminous author," &c.—" Luminous! oh, I meant—*vo*luminous."

Sheridan once said to me, " When posterity read the speeches of Burke, they will hardly be able to believe that, during his life-time, he was not considered as a first-rate speaker, not even as a second-rate one."

When the Duke of York was obliged to retreat before the French, Sheridan gave as a toast, " The Duke of York and his brave followers."

I have seen Sheridan in company with the famous Pamela.* She was lovely—quite radiant with beauty; and Sheridan either was, or pretended to be, violently in love with her. On one occasion I remember that he kept labouring the whole evening at a copy of verses in French, which he intended to present to her, every now and then writing down a word or two on a slip of paper with a pencil. The best of it was, that he understood French very imperfectly.

I prefer Sheridan's *Rivals* to his *School for Scandal*: exquisite humour pleases me more than the finest wit.

* Madame de Genlis's adopted daughter, who was married at Tournay, in 1792, to Lord Edward Fitzgerald. According to Madame de Genlis, in her *Memoirs*, two days before she and Pamela left England, Sheridan declared himself, in her presence, the lover of Pamela, who accepted his hand with pleasure; and it was settled that they should be married—" on our return from France, which was expected to take place in a fortnight." See *Memoirs of Sheridan*, vol. ii. 196, ed. 1827, by Moore, who suspects, not without good reason, that in this affair Sheridan was only amusing himself.

Sheridan was a great artist: what could be more happy in expression than the last of these lines? you may see it illustrated in the Park every Sunday:—

" Hors'd in Cheapside, scarce yet the gayer spark
Achieves the Sunday triumph of the Park;
Scarce yet you see him, dreading to be late,
Scour the New Road and dash through Grosvenor Gate;
Anxious—yet timorous too—his steed to show,
The hack Bucephalus of Rotten Row.
Careless he seems, yet, vigilantly sly,
Woos the stray glance of ladies passing by,
While his off-heel, insidiously aside,
Provokes the caper which he seems to chide."*

I regret that Moore should have printed those memoranda which prove how painfully Sheridan elaborated his compositions; for, though the judicious few will feel that Sheridan was quite right in doing so, the public generally will think the less of him for it.—No wonder that those memoranda were extant: Sheridan was in the habit of putting by, not only all papers written by himself, but all others that came into his hands. Ogle told me that, after his death, he found in his desk sundry unopened letters written by his (Ogle's) mother, who had sent them to Sheridan to be franked.

* Prologue to *Pizarro* (but originally written for, and spoken before, Lady Craven's *Miniature Picture*).

Sheridan did not display his admirable powers in company till he had been warmed by wine. During the earlier part of dinner he was generally heavy and silent; and I have heard him, when invited to drink a glass of wine, reply, " No, thank you; I'll take—a little small beer." After dinner, when he had had a tolerable quantity of wine, he was brilliant indeed. But when he went on swallowing too much, he became downright stupid: and I once, after a dinner-party at the house of Edwards the book-seller in Pall Mall, walked with him to Brookes's, when he had absolutely lost the use of speech.

Sheridan, Sir Walter (then Mr.) Scott, and Moore were one day dining with me, and Sheridan was talking in his very best style, when, to my great vexation, Moore (who has that sort of restlessness which never allows him to be happy where he is) suddenly interrupted Sheridan by exclaiming, " Isn't it time to go to Lydia White's ? "*

During his last illness, the medical attendants apprehending that they would be obliged to perform an operation on him, asked him " if

* Miss Lydia White (long since dead) was an Irish lady of very considerable talents, who gave literary parties, invitations to which were eagerly courted. The following instance of her readiness in reply was communicated to me by my friend the Rev. W. Harness. " At one of Lydia White's small and most agreeable dinners in Park Street, the company (most of them, except the hostess, being Whigs) were discussing in rather a querulous strain the desperate prospects of their party. ' Yes,' said Sydney Smith, ' we are in a most deplorable condition: we must do something to help ourselves; I think we had better sacrifice a Tory virgin.' This was pointedly addressed to Lydia White, who, at once catching and applying the allusion to Iphigenia, answered, ' I believe there is nothing the Whigs would not do *to raise the wind*.' "

he had ever undergone one."—" Never," replied Sheridan, " except when sitting for my picture, or having my hair cut."

Sheridan had very fine eyes, and he was not a little vain of them. He said to me on his death-bed, " Tell Lady Besborough that my eyes will look up to the coffin-lid as brightly as ever."

Soon after his death, Lord Holland wrote a short biographical sketch of him, in which it is stated that he showed during the closing scene a deep sense of devotion. But, on my asking the Bishop of London, who had been called in to read prayers to him, what were the religious feelings of Sheridan in his last moments, the answer was, " I had no means of knowing; for, when I read the prayers, he was totally insensible; Mrs. Sheridan raising him up, and joining his hands together."

In his dealings with the world, Sheridan certainly carried the *privileges of genius* as far as they were ever carried by man.

It is quite true, as stated in several accounts of him, that Fox, when a very young man, was a prodigious dandy,—wearing a little odd French hat, shoes with red heels, &c. He and Lord Carlisle once travelled from Paris to Lyons for the express purpose of buying waistcoats; and during the whole journey they talked about nothing else.

Fox (in his earlier days, I mean), Sheridan, Fitzpatrick, &c., led *such* a life! Lord Tankerville assured me that he has played cards with Fitzpatrick at Brookes's from ten o'clock at night till near six o'clock the next afternoon, a waiter standing by to tell them " whose deal it was," they being too sleepy to know.

After losing large sums at hazard, Fox would go home,—not to destroy himself, as his friends sometimes feared, but—to sit down quietly, and read Greek.

He once won about eight thousand pounds; and one of his bond-creditors, who soon heard of his good luck, presented himself, and asked for payment. " Impossible, sir," replied Fox; " I must first discharge my debts of honour." The bond-creditor remonstrated. " Well, sir, give me your bond." It was delivered to Fox, who tore it in pieces and threw them into the fire. " Now, sir," said Fox, " my debt to you is a debt of honour; " and immediately paid him.

When I became acquainted with Fox, he had given up that kind of life entirely, and resided in the most perfect sobriety and regularity at St. Anne's Hill. There he was very happy, delighting in study, in rural occupations and rural prospects. He would break from a criticism on Porson's *Euripides* to look for the little pigs. I remember his calling out to the Chertsey Hills, when a thick mist, which had for some time concealed them, rolled away, " Good morning to you! I am glad to see you again." There was a walk in his grounds which led to a lane through which the farmers used to pass; and he would stop them, and talk to them, with great interest, about the price of turnips, &c. I was one day with him in the Louvre, when he suddenly turned from the pictures, and, looking out at the window, exclaimed, " This hot sun will burn up my turnips at St. Anne's Hill."

In London mixed society Fox conversed little; but at his own house in the country, with his intimate friends, he would talk on for ever, with all the openness and simplicity of a child: he has continued talking to me for half-an-hour after he had taken up his bed-room candle.—I have seen it somewhere stated that Fox liked to talk about great people: nothing can be more untrue; he hardly ever alluded to them. I remember, indeed, that he once mentioned to me Queen Charlotte, calling her " that bad woman."

He was very shy, and disliked being stared at. Windham and I accompanied him one night to Vauxhall, where he was much annoyed at being followed about, as a spectacle, from place to place. On such occasions he was not only shy, but *gauche*.

One morning at his own house, while speaking to me of his travels, Fox could not recollect the name of a particular town in Holland, and was much vexed at the treacherousness of his memory. He had a dinner-party that day; and, just as he had applied the carving-knife to the sirloin, the name of the town having suddenly occurred to him, he roared out exultingly, to the astonishment of the company, " Gorcum, Gorcum! "

Fox saw Voltaire at Ferney. Their interview was described to me in a letter by Uvedale Price,* who went there with him: but unfortunately I no longer possess that letter; I lent it to Lord Holland, and never could get it back.

It is well known that Fox visited Gibbon at Lausanne; and he was much gratified by the visit. Gibbon, he said, talked a great deal, walking up and down the room, and generally ending his sentences with a genitive case; every now and then, too, casting a look of complacency on his own portrait by Sir Joshua Reynolds, which hung over the chimney-piece,—that wonderful portrait, in which, while the oddness and vulgarity of the features are refined away, the likeness is perfectly preserved.—Fox used to say that Gibbon's *History* was immortal, because nobody could do without it,—nobody, without vast expense of time and labour, could get elsewhere the information which it contains. —I think, and so Lord Grenville thought, that

* An account of the same visit, from the pen of the same writer, occurs in a letter to my unfortunate friend the late E. H. Barker, dated March 24, 1827, from which I shall not scruple to make an extract:—

" From Geneva Fox and I went to Voltaire at Ferney, having obtained a permission then seldom granted. It is an event in one's life to have seen and heard that extraordinary man: he was old and infirm, and, in answer to Fox's note and request, said that the name of Fox was sufficient, and that he could not refuse seeing us, ' *mais que nous venions pour l'exterrer*.' He conversed in a lively manner, walking with us to and fro in a sort of alley; and at parting gave us a list of some of his works, adding, ' *Ce sont des livres de quoi il faut se munir*,' they were such as would fortify our young minds against religious prejudices. Fox quitted us at Geneva, went to England, and commenced his political career."

53

the introductory chapters are the finest part of that history: it was certainly more difficult to write *them* than the rest of the work.

Fox had the highest admiration of Lord North; he considered him a consummate debater. He thought very highly too of Dr. Lawrence's speeches; and said that they only failed in making a deep impression because his manner of delivery was so bad. He disliked Sheridan's famous speeches at Hastings's trial:* yet they fascinated Burke; and to them Fox attributed the change of style which is visible in Burke's later compositions. He did not greatly admire Burke's celebrated *Reflections*.

Never in my life did I hear any thing equal to Fox's *speeches in reply*,—they were wonderful.— Burke did not do himself justice as a speaker: his manner was hurried, and he always seemed to be in a passion.†—Pitt's voice sounded as if he had worsted in his mouth.

Porson said that " Pitt carefully considered his sentences before he uttered them; but that Fox threw himself into the middle of his, and left it to God Almighty to get him out again."

* In Westminster Hall.—It must be remembered, however, that the perhaps more famous speech in the House of Commons, 7th February, 1787, in which Sheridan brought forward against Hastings the charge relative to the Begum Princesses of Oude was publicly eulogised by Fox as a matchless piece of eloquence.

† " Burke," said Mr. Maltby, " always disappointed me as a speaker. I have heard him, during his speeches in the House, make use of the most vulgar expressions, such as ' three nips of a straw,' ' three skips of a louse,' &c.; and, on one occasion when I was present, he introduced, as an illustration, a most indelicate story about a French king who asked his physician why his natural children were so much finer than his legitimate."

Malone was one day walking down Dover Street with Burke, when the latter all at once drew himself up and carried his head aloft with an air of great hauteur. Malone perceived that this was occasioned by the approach of Fox, who presently passed them on the other side of the street. After Fox had gone by, Burke asked Malone very eagerly, " Did he look at me? "

Fox once said to me that " Burke was a most impracticable person, a most unmanageable colleague,—that he never would support any measure, however convinced he might be in his heart of its utility, if it had been first proposed by another ": and he once used these very words, " After all, Burke was a damned wrong-headed fellow, through his whole life jealous and obstinate."

Mrs. Crewe told me that, on some occasion, when it was remarked that Fox still retained his early love for France and every thing French, Burke said, " Yes; he is like a cat,— he is fond of the house, though the family be gone."

I once dined at Mr. Stone's (at Hackney) with Fox, Sheridan, Talleyrand, Madame de Genlis, Pamela, and some other celebrated persons of the time. A natural son of Fox, a dumb boy (who was the very image of his father, and who died a few years after, when about the age of fifteen) was also there, having come, for the occasion, from Braidwood's Academy. To him Fox almost entirely confined his attention, conversing with him by the fingers; and their eyes glistened as they looked at each other. Talleyrand remarked to me, " how strange it was, to dine in company with the first orator in Europe, and only see him *talk with his fingers!* "—That day I offended Madame de Genlis by praising the *Contes Moraux* of Marmontel, with whom she had quarrelled violently.

At a dinner-party, where I was, Fox met Aikin. " I am greatly pleased with your *Miscellaneous Pieces*, Mr. Aikin," said Fox (alluding to the volume written partly by Aikin, and partly by his sister Mrs. Barbauld). Aikin bowed. " I particularly admire," continued Fox, " your essay *Against Inconsistency in our Expectations.*" " That," replied Aikin, " is my sister's."—" I like much," resumed Fox, " your essay *On Monastic Institutions.*" " That," answered Aikin, " is also my sister's." Fox thought it best to say no more about the book.

I was present at a dinner-party given by William Smith in Westminster, when Fox would not take the slightest notice of Horne Tooke,— would not look at him, nor seem to hear any of the good things he said. It was the most painful scene of the kind I was ever witness to, except what occurred at my own house, when the Duke of Wellington treated Lord Holland much in the same way.

At another of Smith's dinners, the conversation turned on Wilberforce; when somebody put the query,—If Wilberforce were compelled to desert either the cause of the slaves, or the party of Mr. Pitt, to which would he adhere? "Oh," said Fox, "he would be for Barabbas." But that was said by Fox merely as a joke; for he greatly respected Pitt; and I remember that, on another occasion at Smith's, when Tierney, &c., endeavoured to persuade Fox that Pitt was not uttering his real sentiments about the abolition of the slave-trade, he would *not* be so persuaded.—Pitt, too, had the highest respect for Fox. One night, after Fox had been speaking, a noble lord, coming out of the House with Pitt, began to abuse Fox's speech. "Don't disparage it," said Pitt; "nobody could have made it but himself."

The Duke of Richmond, Fox, and Burke, were once conversing about history, philosophy, and poetry. The Duke said, "I prefer reading history to philosophy or poetry, because history is *truth*." Both Fox and Burke disagreed with him: they thought that poetry was *truth*, being a representation of human nature: and Fox had some thoughts of writing an essay on the subject.—Lady Glenbervie told me that her father Lord North disliked reading history, because he always doubted its truth.*

In 1792 the Duke of Portland called a meeting of the Whigs at Burlington House, to consider the propriety of their supporting the Proclamation against seditious writings and democratical conspiracies. Francis Duke of Bedford went

* "Thinking to amuse my father once, after his retirement from the ministry, I offered to read a book of history. 'Any thing but history,' said he; 'for history must be false.' "—*Walpoliana*, vol. i. 60.

there. On entering the room, he said to the Duke of Portland, " Is Mr. Fox here? " " No." —" Is he expected here? " " No."—" Then," replied the Duke of Bedford, " I must wish you all good morning "; and immediately withdrew. The Duke of Bedford was stanch to his principles till the hour of his death; and we owe him much.

Fox used to declare of himself that he was " a most painstaking person." When he came into office, finding that his handwriting was very bad, he took lessons to improve it.

He one day pronounced himself to be a bad carver, and, when Mrs. Fox confirmed it, he said, " Yes, my dear, I thought you'd agree with me."

I saw Lunardi make the first ascent in a balloon which had been witnessed in England. It was from the Artillery Ground. Fox was there with his brother General F. The crowd was immense. Fox, happening to put his hand down to his watch, found another hand upon it, which he immediately seized. " My friend," said he to the owner of the strange hand, " you have chosen an occupation which will be your ruin at last." " O, Mr. Fox," was the reply, " forgive me, and let me go! I have been driven to this course by necessity alone; my wife and children are starving at home." Fox, always tender-hearted, slipped a guinea into the hand, and then released it. On the conclusion of the show, Fox was proceeding to look what o'clock it was. " Good God," cried he,

" my watch is gone! " " Yes," answered General F., " I know it is; I saw your friend take it."—" Saw him take it! and you made no attempt to stop him? " " Really, you and he appeared to be on such good terms with each other, that I did not choose to interfere."

I was walking through the Louvre with Fox, when he all but *cut* Mackintosh, passing him with a nod and a " How d'ye do? " and he gave me to understand that he had done so because he was angry at Mackintosh for having accepted a place in India from the Tories. Fitzpatrick, however, told me the real cause of Fox's anger; and it was this;—Mrs. Mackintosh had not called upon Mrs. Fox, whom Fox had recently acknowledged as his wife. Such slight things sometimes influence the conduct of great men.

Most unfortunately, one morning during breakfast at St. Anne's Hill, I repeated and praised Goldsmith's song, " When lovely woman stoops to folly," &c., quite forgetting that it must necessarily hurt the feelings of Mrs. Fox. She seemed a good deal discomposed by it. Fox merely remarked, " Some people write damned nonsense."

When Buonaparte said to Fox, he was convinced that Windham was implicated in the contrivance of the Infernal Machine, Fox warmly repelled such an aspersion on Windham's character, assuring the First Consul that no Englishman would degrade himself by being concerned in so vile a business.—I told this to Windham, who answered very coldly, " Well, I should have said the same of him under similar circumstances."—I have heard Windham speak very disrespectfully of Fox in the House, after their political quarrel.

Fox said that Sir Joshua Reynolds never enjoyed Richmond,*—that he used to say the human face was *his* landscape. Fox did not much admire Sir Joshua's pictures in the grand style; he greatly preferred those of a playful character: he did not like much even the Ugolino; but he thought the boys in the Nativity were charming.

Once, at Paris, talking to Fox about Le Sueur's pictures, I said that I doubted if any artist had ever excelled Le Sueur in painting *white garments*. Fox replied that he thought Andrea Sacchi superior to Le Sueur in that respect. I mention this to show that Fox was not only fond of painting, but had given minute attention to it.

He was an eager chess-player: I have heard him say, on coming down to breakfast, that he had not been able to sleep for thinking about some particular move.

While young Betty was in all his glory, I went with Fox and Mrs. Fox, after dining with them in Arlington Street, to see him act Hamlet; and, during the play-scene, Fox, to my infinite

* Where Reynolds had a villa.—In Mr. Rogers's collection of pictures was an exquisite landscape by Sir Joshua,—a view from Richmond Hill, with the features of the scene a little altered.

surprise, said, " This is finer than Garrick."*—
How wise it was in Kemble and Mrs. Siddons
quietly to withdraw from the stage during the
Betty furor, and then as quietly to return to it,
as if nothing unusual had occurred!

Fox said that Barry's Romeo was superior to
Garrick's.

" If I had a son," observed Fox, " I should
insist on his frequently writing English verses,
whether he had a taste for poetry or not, because
that sort of composition forces one to consider
very carefully the exact meanings of words."

I introduced Wordsworth to Fox, having
taken him with me to a ball given by Mrs. Fox.
" I am very glad to see you, Mr. Wordsworth,
though I am not of your faction," was all that
Fox said to him,—meaning that he admired a
school of poetry different from that to which
Wordsworth belonged.

Fox considered Burnet's style to be perfect.
We were once talking of an historian's introducing occasionally the words of other writers
into his work without marking them as quotations, when Fox said, " that the style of some
of the authors so treated might need a little
mending, but that Burnet's required none."

* Such criticism will now seem (and undoubtedly is) preposterous.
But we must recollect that there was a marvellous charm about the
young Roscius.—" Northcote then spoke of the boy, as he always
calls him (Master Betty). He asked if I had ever seen him act; and
I said, Yes, and was one of his admirers. He answered, ' Oh! yes,
it was such a beautiful effusion of natural sensibility; and then that
graceful play of the limbs in youth gave such an advantage over
every one about him.' Humphreys (the artist) said, ' He had never
seen the little Apollo off the pedestal before.' "—Hazlitt's *Conversations of Northcote*, p. 23.

He was so fond of Dryden, that he had some idea of editing his works. It was absurd, he said, not to print the originals by Chaucer along with Dryden's versions of them; and absurd in Malone to print all Dryden's Prefaces by themselves. "Dryden's imitations of Horace," he would say, "are better than the originals: how fine this is!—

' Happy the man, and happy he alone,
   He who can call to-day his own;
   He who, secure within, can say,
To-morrow, do thy worst, for I have liv'd to-day;
   Be fair or foul, or rain or shine,
The joys I have possess'd, in spite of Fate, are
     mine;
   Not Heaven itself upon the past has power,
But what has been, has been, and I have had
     my hour.' "*

One forenoon, at his own house, Fox was talking to me very earnestly about Dryden, when he suddenly recollected that (being in office) he ought to make his appearance at the King's levee. It was so late that, not having time to change his dress, he set off for court "accoutred as he was"; and when somebody remarked to him that his coat was not quite the thing, he replied, "No matter; *he* [i.e. George the Third] is so blind that he can't distinguish what I have on."

There was a period of his life when Fox used

* *Twenty-ninth Ode of the First Book of Horace paraphrased, &c.*

to say that he could not forgive Milton for having occasioned him the trouble of reading through a poem (*Paradise Lost*), three parts of which were not worth reading. He afterwards, however, estimated it more justly. Milton's prose works he never could endure.

He said that Mrs. Sheridan's *Sidney Biddulph* was the best of all modern novels. (By the by, Sheridan used to declare that *he* had never read it!*)

When Fox was a young man, a copy of Massinger accidentally fell into his hands: he read it, and, for some time after, could talk of nothing but Massinger.

He thought so highly of the *Isacco* of Metastasio, that he considered it as one of the four most beautiful compositions produced during the century; the other three being Pope's *Eloisa to Abelard*, Voltaire's *Zaire*, and Gray's *Elegy*.†

" No one," said Fox, " could be an ill-tempered man who wrote so much nonsense as Swift did."

His admiration of Ariosto was extreme.—He thought Petrarch's Latin letters better than his Sonnets.

He once pointed out to me, as excellent, this passage of Paley. " The distinctions of civil life are almost always insisted upon too much, and urged too far. Whatever, therefore,

* The incident, in *The School for Scandal*, of Sir Oliver's presenting himself to his relations in disguise, is manifestly taken by Sheridan from his mother's novel.

† Yet, we have been told, Fox did not consider the *Elegy* as Gray's best poem: see p. 23.

conduces to restore the level, by qualifying the dispositions which grow out of great elevation or depression of rank, improves the character on both sides. Now things are made to appear little by being placed beside what is great. In which manner, superiorities, that occupy the whole field of the imagination, will vanish or shrink to their proper diminutiveness, when compared with the distance by which even the highest of men are removed from the Supreme being, and this comparison is naturally introduced by all acts of joint worship. If ever the poor man holds up his head, it is at church: if ever the rich man views him with respect, it is there: and both will be the better, and the public profited, the oftener they meet in a situation, in which the consciousness of dignity in the one is tempered and mitigated, and the spirit of the other erected and confirmed."*

Fox used to read Homer through once every year. On my asking him, " Which poem had you rather have written, the *Iliad* or the *Odyssey?* " he answered, " I know which I had rather read " (meaning the *Odyssey*).

Euripides was his grand favourite among the Greek poets. He fancied that Shakespeare must have met with some translation of Euripides, for he could trace resemblances between passages of their dramas: *e.g.* what Alcestis in her last moments says about her servants is like what the dying Queen Katharine (in *Henry the Eighth*) says about hers, &c.

* *Mor. and Pol. Philosophy*, b. v. ch. 4.

He considered the *Œdipus Coloneus* as the best play of Sophocles; and he admired greatly his *Electra*.

He did not much like Cæsar's *Commentaries;* they appeared to him rather dry, and deficient in thought. He said that the letter to Oppius and Balbus, which is very little known, was the piece that did Cæsar most honour; and that he had once transcribed it with the intention of sending it to Buonaparte, when the news of the Duke d'Enghien's death made him change his mind.

He observed that the Greek historians generally told nothing but truth, while the Latin historians generally told nothing but lies.

He was a constant reader of Virgil; and had been so from a very early period. There is at Holland House a copy of Virgil covered with Fox's manuscript notes, written when he was a boy, and expressing the most enthusiastic admiration of that poet.

He once told me that the extracts which he had seen from Hippocrates had given him a high opinion of that writer;—that one of his aphorisms was excellent,—" The second-best remedy is better than the best, if the patient likes it best; "—and that he intended to read his works.

Afterwards, calling upon him in Stable Yard when he happened to be ill, I found him reading Hippocrates.—On that occasion I said I wished that the new administration would put down the east wind by an Act of Parliament. He replied, smiling (and waking, as it were, from one of his fits of torpor), that they would find it difficult to do *that*, but that they would do as much good in that as they would in any thing else.

He said that *Lear*, *Othello*, and *Macbeth* were the best of Shakespeare's works; that the first act of *Hamlet* was pre-eminent; that the ghost in that play was quite unequalled,—there was nothing like it; and that Hamlet was *not* mad.— On another occasion he said that the character of Macbeth was very striking and original,— that at first he is an object of our pity, and that he becomes gradually worse and worse, till at last he has no virtue left except courage.

He thought Raleigh a very fine writer. Bolingbroke he did not like. Surrey was " too old " for him.

He said that Congreve's *Way of the World* was a charming comedy, but his *Mourning Bride* altogether execrable; that Sheridan's *Pizarro* was the worst thing possible.

He had never been able to read Mickle's *Lusiad* through. He once met Mickle, and took a dislike to him.

He was fond of the song, " The heavy hours are almost past," by Lord Lyttelton; whose son, he said, was a very bad man,—downright wicked.

He thought Mrs. Barbauld's *Life of Richardson* admirable; and regretted that she wasted her talents in writing books for children (excellent as those books might be), now that there were so many pieces of that description.

The Adventurer, he said, was very poor; *The World* far superior, and he had read it with pleasure.

He thought Tickell's* lines *On the Death of Addison* quite perfect; and he liked a large portion of his *Kensington Gardens*.

He often spoke with high praise of Cowper's *Epistle to Joseph Hill*. It was through Windham that he first became acquainted with Cowper's poetry.

Very shortly before he died, he complained of great uneasiness in his stomach; and Cline† advised him to try the effects of a cup of coffee. It was accordingly ordered: but, not being brought so soon as was expected, Mrs. Fox expressed some impatience; upon which Fox said, with his usual sweet smile, " Remember, my dear, that good coffee cannot be made in a moment."

Lady Holland announced the death of Fox in her own odd manner to those relatives and intimate friends of his who were sitting in a room near his bed-chamber, and waiting to hear that he had breathed his last;—she walked through the room with her apron thrown over her head.

Trotter's *Memoirs of Fox*, though incorrect in some particulars, is a very pleasing book. Trotter died in Ireland: he was reduced to great straits; and Mrs. Fox sent him, at different

---

* " Tickell's merit," Wordsworth remarked to me, " is not sufficiently known. I think him one of the very best writers of occasional verses."

† The surgeon.—*Ed.*

times, as much as several hundred pounds, though she could ill spare the money.

How fondly the surviving friends of Fox cherished his memory! Many years after his death, I was at a fête given by the Duke of Devonshire at Chiswick House. Sir Robert Adair and I wandered about the apartments. " In which room did Fox expire? " asked Adair. I replied, " In this very room." Immediately Adair burst into tears with a vehemence of grief such as I hardly ever saw exhibited by a man.

Fox's *History of the Early Part of the Reign of James the Second* has been greatly undervalued; but it will be properly estimated in future times. It contains charming passages. When I read them, I seem to listen to Fox conversing.

Burke said to Mrs. Crewe: " A dull proser is more endurable than a dull joker."

He also said to her: " England is a moon shone upon by France. France has all things within herself; and she possesses the power of recovering from the severest blows. England is an artificial country: take away her commerce, and what has she? "

One day Foote was taken in to White's by a friend who wanted to write a note. Foote, standing in a room among strangers, appeared to feel not quite at ease. Lord Carmarthen, wishing to relieve his embarrassment, came up to speak to him; but, himself, feeling rather shy, he merely said, " Mr. Foote, your hand-kerchief is hanging out of your pocket." Upon which, Foote, looking suspiciously round, and hurriedly thrusting the handkerchief back into his pocket, replied, " Thank you, my lord; you know the company better than I do."

Fox told me that Lord William Bentinck once invited Foote to meet him and some others at dinner in St. James's Street; and that they were rather angry at Lord William for having done so, expecting that Foote would prove only a bore, and a check on their conversation. " But," said Fox, " we soon found that we were mistaken: whatever we talked about,—whether fox-hunt-ing, the turf, or any other subject,—Foote instantly took the lead, and delighted us all."

Murphy, who used to dwell with enthusiasm on his recollections of Chatham's oratory, was once in the gallery of the House with Foote, when Pitt (Lord Chatham) was putting forth all his power in an attack on Murray (Lord Mansfield). " Shall we go home now? " said Murphy.—" No," replied Foote; " let us wait till he has made the little man (Murray) vanish entirely."

There was no end to Foote's jokes about Garrick's parsimony. " Garrick," said Foote, " lately invited Hurd to dine with him in the Adelphi; and after dinner, the evening being very warm, they walked up and down in front of the house. As they passed and re-passed the dining-room windows, Garrick was in a perfect agony; for he saw that there was a thief in one of the candles which were burning on the table; and yet Hurd was a person of such consequence that he could not run away from him to prevent the waste of his tallow."

At the Chapter Coffee-house, Foote and his friends were making a contribution for the relief of a poor fellow (a decayed player, I believe), who was nick-named the Captain of the Four Winds, because his hat was worn into four spouts. Each person of the company dropped his mite into the hat, as it was held out to him. " If Garrick hears of this," said Foote, " he will certainly send us *his* hat."

The then Duke of Cumberland (the *foolish* Duke, as he was called) came one night into Foote's green-room at the Haymarket Theatre. " Well, Foote," said he, " here I am, ready, as usual, to swallow all your good things."— " Upon my soul," replied Foote, " your Royal Highness must have an excellent digestion, for you never bring any up again."

During my youth I used to go to the Hampstead Assemblies, which were frequented by a great deal of good company. There I have danced four or five minuets in one evening.

Beau Nash was once dancing a minuet at Bath with a Miss Lunn. She was so long of giving him *both her hands* (the figure by which the lady, when she thinks proper, brings the

SAMUEL ROGERS
with the Hon. Mrs. Norton and Mrs. Phipps
from the painting by F. Stone A.R.A.

performance to a close), that he lost all patience, and, suiting the words to the tune (which was *Marshal Saxe's minuet*), he sung out, as she passed him,—

> " Miss Lunn, Miss Lunn,
> Will you never have done ? "

I always distrust the accounts of eminent men by their *contemporaries*. None of us has any reason to slander Homer or Julius Cæsar; but we find it very difficult to divest ourselves of prejudices when we are writing about persons with whom we have been acquainted.

Lord St. Helens (who had been ambassador to Russia) told me, as a fact, this anecdote of the Empress Catherine. She frequently had little whist-parties, at which she sometimes played, and sometimes not. One night, when she was not playing, but walking about from table to table, and watching the different hands, she rang the bell to summon the page-in-waiting from an ante-chamber. No page appeared. She rang the bell again; and again without effect. Upon this, she left the room, looking daggers, and did not return for a very considerable time; the company supposing that the unfortunate page was destined to the knout or Siberia. On entering the ante-chamber, the Empress found that the page, like his betters, was busy at whist, and that, when she had rung the bell, he happened to have so very interesting a hand that he could not make up his mind to quit it. Now, what did the Empress do? she despatched the page on her errand, and then quietly sat down to hold his cards till he should return.

Lord St. Helens also told me that he and Ségur were with the Empress in her carriage, when the horses took fright, and ran furiously down hill. The danger was excessive. When it was over, the Empress said, " Mon étoile vous a sauvée."

Hare's wit, once so famous, owed perhaps not a little to his manner of uttering it. Here is a specimen. Fox was sitting at Brookes's, in a very moody humour, having lost a considerable sum at cards, and was indolently moving a pen backwards and forwards over a sheet of paper. " What is he drawing? " said some one to Hare. " Any thing but a draft," was the reply.

General Fitzpatrick was at one time nearly as famous for his wit as Hare. During the latter part of his long life he had withdrawn a good deal from society. I took farewell of him the day but one before he died. On the day immediately preceding his death, I walked to his house in Arlington Street to inquire for him; and, just as I reached the door, Mrs. Fox was coming from it, sobbing violently.

Jekyll, too, was celebrated for his wit; but it was of that kind which amuses only for the moment. I remember that when Lady Cork gave a party at which she wore a most enormous plume, Jekyll said, " She was exactly a shuttle-cock,—all *cork* and feathers."

While Rousseau was lodging in Chiswick Terrace, Fitzpatrick called upon him one day, and had not been long in the room when David Hume entered. Rousseau had lost a favourite dog; and Hume, having exerted himself to recover it, now brought it back to its master, who thanked him with expressions of the most fervent gratitude, and shed tears of joy over the animal.

Fitzpatrick, who had been much in the company of David Hume, used always to speak of him as " a delicious creature."

Hume told Cadell the bookseller that he had a great desire to be introduced to as many of the persons who had written against him as could be collected; and requested Cadell to bring him and them together. Accordingly, Dr. Douglas, Dr. Adams, &c. &c., were invited by Cadell to dine at his house in order to meet Hume. They came; and Dr. Price, who was of the party, assured me that they were all delighted with David.

I knew Murphy long and intimately: I was introduced to him by the Piozzis at Streatham.

On the first night of any of his plays, if the slightest symptoms of disapprobation were shown by the audience, Murphy always left the house, and took a walk in Covent-Garden Market: then, after having composed himself, he would return to the theatre.

Garrick once, in conversation with Murphy, having insisted that it was much more difficult to write a play whose strength lay in the plot than one which depended on the dialogue for its effect, Murphy went to his favourite haunt, The Talbot at Richmond, and wrote, nearly at a single sitting, a comedy of the former description (I forget its name), which, very soon after, he presented to Garrick.

The days had been when Murphy lived in the best society, and used to walk about arm-in-arm with Lord Loughborough: but I have seen them meet in the street, and salute each other very formally.

Towards the close of his life, till he received a pension of 200*l.* per annum from the king, Murphy was in great pecuniary difficulties. He had eaten himself out of every tavern from the other side of Temple-Bar to the west end of the town. I have still in my possession several bills of his for money to a considerable amount which he never repaid me.—He had borrowed from me two hundred pounds; and a long time having elapsed without his taking any notice of the debt, I became rather uneasy (for two hundred pounds was then no trifling sum to me). At last, meeting him in Fleet Street, I asked him when he should be able to settle with me. "Are you going home?" said he. "Yes," I replied; and we walked to my chambers in the Temple. There, instead of making any arrangements for repaying me, he exerted all his eloquence, but in vain, to induce me to lend him more money; and I thanked heaven when I got rid of him.—He assigned over to me the whole of his works, including his Tacitus; and I soon found that he had already disposed of them to a bookseller! For this transaction Murphy came, in extreme agitation, to offer me a sort of apology, almost throwing himself on his knees. When he made his appearance, Porson and Maltby happened to be in the room; but, Porson having said aside to Maltby, "*We* had better withdraw," they left me to my disagreeable conference with Murphy.

One thing ought to be remembered to Murphy's honour: an actress,* with whom he had lived, bequeathed to him all her property, but he gave up every farthing of it to her relations.

Murphy used to say that there were Four Estates in England, the King, the Lords, the Commons, and—*the Theatres*. He certainly would not say so, if he were alive now, when the national theatre is almost extinct.

Henderson was a truly great actor ; his Hamlet and his Falstaff were equally good. He was a very fine reader too; in his comic readings

* Miss Elliot.

superior, of course, to Mrs. Siddons; his *John Gilpin* was marvellous.

He would frequently produce very unexpected " effects " in his readings: for instance, in the passage of Collins's *Ode to Fear*,—

> " Or throws him on the ridgy steep
> Of some loose-hanging rock to sleep; "—

he would suddenly pause after the words " loose-hanging rock," and then, starting back as if in amazement, and lifting his arms above his head, he would slowly add—" to sleep! "

During his boyhood, Pitt was very weakly; and his physician, Addington (Lord Sidmouth's father), ordered him to take port wine in large quantities: the consequence was, that, when he grew up, he could not do without it. Lord Grenville has seen him swallow a bottle of port in tumblerfuls, before going to the House. This, together with his habit of eating late suppers (indigestible cold veal-pies,* &c.), helped undoubtedly to shorten his life. Huskisson, speaking to me of Pitt, said that his hands shook so much, that, when he helped himself to salt, he was obliged to support the right hand with the left.

Stothard the painter happened to be one evening at an inn on the Kent Road, when Pitt and Dundas put up there on their way from

---

* One version of Pitt's last words is: " I think I could eat one of Bellamy's pork-pies."—*Ed.*

Walmer. Next morning, as they were stepping into their carriage, the waiter said to Stothard, " Sir, do you observe these two gentlemen? " " Yes," he replied; " and I know them to be Mr. Pitt and Mr. Dundas."—" Well, sir, how much wine do you suppose they drank last night? " Stothard could not guess. " Seven bottles, sir."

Lord Grenville once said to Pitt, " I am really astonished at your fluency in public speaking: how was it acquired? " He replied, " I believe it may be attributed to this circumstance: when I was a lad, my father used every evening to make me translate freely, before him and the rest of the family, those portions of Livy, Virgil, &c., which I had read in the morning with my tutor, Mr. Wilson."—Lord Grenville engaged a reporter to take down Pitt's speeches; but the reporter completely failed.

Pitt had been accustomed when a boy to go a-bird-nesting at Holwood, and hence (according to Lord Grenville) his wish to possess that place; which he eventually did.

I was assured by Lord Grenville that Pitt came into office with a fixed determination to improve the finances of the kingdom; instead of which he greatly injured them.

I don't remember having heard of any *bon-mots* being uttered by Pitt in society; and those persons who were very intimate with him could tell me little in favour of his conversational powers: one great lady who knew him well, said that he was generally quite silent in company;

and a second could give me no other information about him, but that (being a tall man) " he sat very high at table! "

There was a run on the Bank of England, and Pitt was uncertain what measures to take in consequence of it. He passed the whole night (as Mrs. —— told me) in walking up and down his drawing-room. Next morning he sent for certain bankers, and informed them that he had resolved on authorising the Bank to suspend cash-payments, and to stop the issue of gold.— I recollect a farmer coming to my father's bank, and receiving his money in five-pound notes. " What can I do with these? " he exclaimed; " how can I pay my men with them? "

Wilberforce requested Pitt to read Butler's *Analogy*.* Pitt did so; and was by no means satisfied with the reasoning in it. " My dear Wilberforce," he said, " you may prove *any thing* by analogy."

Combe, author of *The Diaboliad*, of *Lord Lyttelton's Letters*, and, more recently, of *Doctor Syntax's Three Tours*, was a most extraordinary person. During a very long life, he had seen much of the world,—its ups and downs. He was certainly well-connected. Fitzpatrick

* " One evening, at a party, when Butler's *Analogy* was mentioned, Parr said in his usual pompous manner, ' I shall not declare, before the present company, my opinion of that book.' Bowles, who was just then leaving the room, muttered, ' Nobody cares what you think of it.' Parr, overhearing him, roared out, ' What's that you say, Bowles? ' and added, as the door shut on the offender, ' It's lucky that Bowles is gone! for I should have put him to death.' "— *Maltby*.

recollected him at Douay College.* He moved once in the highest society, and was very intimate with the Duke of Bedford. Twenty thousand pounds were unexpectedly bequeathed to him by an old gentleman, who said "he ought to have been Combe's father" (that is, he had been on the point of marrying Combe's mother), and who therefore left him that large sum. Combe contrived to get rid of the money in an incredibly short time.

Combe was staying at the house of Uvedale Price;† and the Honourable Mr. St. John (author of *Mary Queen of Scots*‡) was there also. The latter, one morning, missed some banknotes. Price, strongly suspecting who had taken them, mentioned the circumstance to Combe, and added, " Perhaps it would be as well if you cut short your visit here." " Oh, certainly," replied Combe with the greatest coolness; " and allow me just to ask, whether henceforth we are to be friends or acquaintances? "—" Acquaintances, if you please," said Price.—Long after this had happened, I was passing through Leicester Square with Price, when we met Combe: we both spoke to him; but from that hour he always avoided me.

* According to *The Gentleman's Magazine* for August 1823, p. 185 (where his name is wrongly spelled *Coombe*), " he was educated at Eton and Oxford: " which is not inconsistent with his having been at Douay also. But there seems to be great uncertainty about the particulars of his life.

† Sir Uvedale Price, author of *Essays on the Picturesque.—Ed.*

‡ A very dull tragedy, in which Mrs. Siddons continued to act the heroine occasionally up to the time of her retirement from the stage. I recollect her performing Mary at Edinburgh during my boyhood.

Combe assured me that it was with him, not with Sterne, that " Eliza "* was in love; that he used to meet her often beside a windmill near Brighton; that he was once surprised in her bed-chamber, and fled through the window, leaving one of his shoes behind him; that, some days after, he encountered her as she was walking with a party on what is now the Steyne (at Brighton), and that, as she passed him, she displayed from her muff the toe of his shoe!

Combe died in the King's Bench,† where it was said that he had taken refuge in order to cheat his creditors,—erroneously, for he did not leave enough to pay the expenses of his funeral.

Gibbon took very little exercise. He had been staying some time with Lord Sheffield in the country; and when he was about to go away, the servants could not find his hat. " Bless me," said Gibbon, " I certainly left it in the hall on my arrival here." He had not stirred out of doors during the whole of the visit.

These lines by Bishop (Head-master of Merchant-Tailors' School) are very good in their way:—

* A list of Combe's writings, drawn up by himself, and printed in *The Gentleman's Magazine* for May 1852, p. 467, includes " Letters supposed to have passed between Sterne and Eliza, 2 vols."

† He died June 19th, 1823, at his apartments in Lambeth Road, in his 82nd year. See *The Gentleman's Magazine* for August 1823, p. 185.

" To Mrs. Bishop, with a Present of a Knife.

' A knife,' dear girl, ' cuts love,' they say!
Mere modish love perhaps it may;
For any tool, of any kind,
Can separate—what was never join'd.

The knife that cuts our love in two
Will have much tougher work to do;
Must cut your softness, truth, and spirit,
Down to the vulgar size of merit;
To level yours with modern taste,
Must cut a world of sense to waste;
And from your single beauty's store
Clip what would dizen out a score.

That self-same blade from me must sever
Sensation, judgment, sight, for ever;
All memory of endearments past,
All hope of comforts long to last;
All that makes fourteen years with you
A summer,—and a short one too;
All that affection feels and fears,
When hours without you seem like years.

Till that be done (and I'd as soon
Believe this knife will chip the moon),
Accept my present, undeterr'd,
And leave their proverbs to the herd.

If in a kiss—delicious treat!—
Your lips acknowledge the receipt,
Love, fond of such substantial fare,
And proud to play the glutton there,
All thoughts of cutting will disdain,
Save only—' cut and come again.' "

I never saw Paley; but my brother knew him well, and liked him much. Paley used to say, in his broad dialect, " I am an advocate for corr*oo*ption " (that is, parliamentary influence).*

Witticisms are often attributed to the wrong people. It was Lord Chesterfield, not Sheridan, who said, on occasion of a certain marriage, that " Nobody's son had married Everybody's daughter."

Lord Chesterfield remarked of two persons dancing a minuet, that " they looked as if they were hired to do it, and were doubtful of being paid."

I once observed to a Scotch lady, " how desirable it was in any danger *to have presence of mind*." " I had rather," she rejoined, " *have absence of body*."

* Among several anecdotes of Paley, communicated to me long ago by a gentleman who resided in his neighbourhood, were these.— When Paley rose in the church, he set up a carriage, and, by his wife's directions, his arms were painted on the panels. They were copied from the engraving on a silver cup, which Mrs. P. supposed to be the bearings of his family. Paley thought it a pity to undeceive his wife; but the truth was, he had purchased the cup at a sale.

He permitted,—nay, wished,—his daughters to go to evening parties; but insisted that one of them should always remain at home, to give her assistance, if needed, by rubbing him, &c., in case of an attack of the rheumatic pains to which he was subject. " This," he said, " taught them natural affection."

His fourth son chose to be a farmer, and was sent by his father to Redburn, where, in order to train him to his business, he was frequently employed in works of manual labour. A friend, having seen the young man so occupied, expressed his surprise at the circumstance to Paley, who replied, " Practice, practice is every thing."

The *méchant* Lord Lyttelton used to play all sorts of tricks in his boyhood. For instance, when he knew that the larder at Hagley happened to be ill supplied, he would invite, in his father's name, a large party to dinner; and, as the carriages drove up the avenue, the old lord (concealing his vexation as much as possible) would stand bowing in the hall, to welcome his unwelcome guests.

There is at Hagley a written account of the *méchant* Lord Lyttelton's death, which was read to me while on a visit there. The statement, as far as I recollect, runs thus.—One night, when he was in bed, a white bird, with a voice like a woman's,—or else, a female figure with a bird on her hand,—appeared to him, and told him that he must die at a particular hour on a particular night. He related the circumstance to some of his friends, who encouraged him in treating it as a delusion. The fatal night arrived. He was then at a house (Pitt Place) near Epsom; and had appointed to meet a party on the downs next morning. His friends, without his knowledge, had put back the clock. " I shall cheat the ghost yet," he said. On getting into bed, he sent his servant down stairs for a spoon, having to take some medicine. When the servant returned, Lord Lyttelton was a corpse.*

* In the " Corrections and Additions," p. 36, to Nash's *History of Worcestershire*, is an account of Lord Lyttelton's vision and death, more detailed than the above, but not materially different.

Of Lord Lyttelton's ghost appearing to Miles Peter Andrews (an anecdote quite as notorious as that above) the following account
(*continued on next page*)

Frequently, when doubtful how to act in matters of importance, I have received more useful advice from women than from men. Women have the understanding *of the heart;* which is better than that of the head.

As I was walking home one day from my father's bank, I observed a great crowd of people streaming into a chapel in the City Road. I followed them; and saw laid out, upon a table, the dead body of a clergyman in full canonicals; his gray hair partly shading his face on both sides, and his flesh resembling wax. It was the corpse of John Wesley; and the crowd moved slowly and silently round and round the table, to take a last look at that most venerable man.*

(*continued from previous page*)
was given by Andrews himself to his most intimate friend, Mr. Morton the dramatist, by whom it was told to me. " I was at Richmond: and I had not been long in bed, when I saw Lord Lyttelton standing at the foot of it. I felt no surprise, because he was in the habit of coming to me at all hours without previous announcement. I spoke to him; but he did not answer. Supposing that he intended, as usual, to play me some trick, I stooped out of bed, and taking up one of my slippers, I threw it at him. He vanished. Next morning, I inquired of the people of the house when Lord Lyttelton had arrived, and where he was ? They declared that he had *not* arrived. He died at the very moment I saw him." A version of this ghost-story, too, is given by Nash (*ubi supra*), who states that Andrews addressed the ghost, and that " the ghost, shaking his head, said, ' It is all over with me.' " But Mr. Morton assured me that he related the story *exactly as he had had it from Andrews,* whose conviction that he had seen a real spectre was proof against all arguments.

* Since the first edition of the present volume was printed, a letter has appeared in *The Gentleman's Magazine* for February, 1856, where (p. 148) the writer states that Mr. Rogers, *very late in*
(*continued on next page*)

Dr. Priestley went to Paris in company with Lord Shelburne;* and he assured me that all the eminent Frenchmen whom he met there were entirely destitute of any religious belief,—sheer atheists. At a large dinner-party he asked his next neighbour, " Who is that gentleman? " The answer was, " It is ——; and he believes no more *than you and I do.*"†—Marmontel used to read some of his unpublished works to parties of his friends, on certain days, at his own house. Priestley, who attended a few of those readings, declared that Marmontel occasionally gesticulated with such violence, that it was necessary to keep out of the reach of his arms for fear of being knocked down.

(continued from previous page)
life, mentioned to him this anecdote, with the important variation—that the body of Wesley was lying *in the drawing-room of a house to the left of the chapel.* But, *towards the close of his career,* Mr. Rogers's memory was not to be trusted to for minute particulars.—" At the desire of many friends his corpse was placed in the New Chapel, and remained there the day before his interment," &c. Coke and Moore's *Life of Wesley,* p. 511.—" At the desire of many of his friends, his body was carried into the chapel the day preceding the interment, and there lay in a kind of state becoming the person, dressed in his clerical habit, with gown, cassock, and band; the old clerical cap on his head, a Bible in one hand, and a white handkerchief in the other. The face was placid, and the expression which death had fixed upon his venerable features was that of a serene and heavenly smile. The crowds who flocked to see him were so great, that it was thought prudent, for fear of accidents, to accelerate the funeral, and perform it between five and six in the morning," &c.—Southey's *Life of Wesley,* ii, 562, ed. 1820. Wesley died 2nd March, 1791.

* Afterwards Marquis of Lansdowne,—to whom, nominally, Priestley acted as librarian, but really as his literary companion. It was in 1774 that they made a tour to the Continent.

† Clayden's *Early Life of S.R.* gives further point to this story by revealing that the two gentlemen in question were the Bishop of Aix and the Archbishop of Toulouse.—*Ed.*

I was intimately acquainted with Dr. Priestley; and a more amiable man never lived; he was all gentleness, kindness, and humility. He was once dining with me, when some one asked him (rather rudely) " how many books he had published? " He replied, " Many more, sir, than I should like to read." Before going to America, he paid me a visit, passing a night at my house. He left England chiefly in compliance with the wishes of his wife.

When Horne Tooke was at school, the boys asked him " what his father was? " Tooke answered, " A Turkey merchant." (He was a poulterer.)

He once said to his brother, a pompous man, " You and I have reversed the natural course of things : you have risen by your gravity; I have sunk by my levity."

To Judge Ashhurst's remark, that the law was open to all, both to the rich and to the poor, Tooke replied, " So is the London Tavern."

He said that Hume wrote his History as witches say their prayers—backwards.

Tooke told me that in his early days a friend gave him a letter of introduction to D'Alembert at Paris. Dressed *à-la-mode*, he presented the letter, and was very courteously received by D'Alembert, who talked to him about operas, comedies, and suppers, &c. Tooke had expected conversation on very different topics, and was greatly disappointed. When he took leave, he was followed by a gentleman in a plain suit, who had been in the room during his interview with D'Alembert, and who had perceived his chagrin. " D'Alembert," said the gentleman, " supposed from your gay apparel that you were merely a *petit maitre*." The gentleman was David Hume. On his next visit to D'Alembert, Tooke's dress was altogether different; and so was the conversation.*

Tooke went to Italy as tutor to a young man of fortune,† who was subject to fits of insanity, and who consequently would sometimes occasion much alarm at inns during the middle of the night.—While residing at Genoa, they formed an acquaintance with an Italian family of distinction, by whom they were introduced to the best society of the place. Tooke attached himself to a lady of great beauty, becoming her *cavalier servente*, and attending her every where. After some weeks, at a large evening party, he was astonished to find that the lady would not speak to him, and that the rest of the company avoided conversation with him. " Now," said Tooke, " what do you imagine was the cause of this? Why, they had discovered *that I was a*

* Tooke spent considerably more than a year at Paris, while acting as travelling-tutor to young Elwes (son of the miser); and he afterwards paid two short visits to that capital in company with young Taylor (see next note). It was, I apprehend, on the first of these occasions that his introduction to D'Alembert took place. He was in full orders before he ever went to the Continent; but he always laid aside the clerical dress at Dover.

† The son of a Mr. Taylor, who resided within a few miles of Brentford.

Protestant clergyman! But I was resolved not to be brow-beaten; and I made myself so agreeable, that, before the party broke up, we were all again on the very best terms; some of them even waited on me home, with music, in a sort of triumph! "*

Soon after Tooke had left Genoa, he heard that another traveller, who was following the same route, had been assassinated. This unfortunate traveller was mistaken for Tooke, on whom, in consequence of his intrigue with the lady at Genoa, the blow had been intended to fall.

I have been present when one of Tooke's daughters was reading Greek† to him with great facility. He had made her learn that language without using a grammar,—only a dictionary.

I paid five guineas (in conjunction with Boddington) for a *loge* at Tooke's trial.—It was the custom in those days (and perhaps is so still) to place bunches of strong-smelling plants of different sorts at the bar where the criminal was to sit (I suppose, to purify the air from the contagion of his presence!). This was done at Tooke's trial; but, as soon as he was brought in, he indignantly swept them away with his handkerchief. The trial lasted six days. Erskine (than whom nobody had ever more power over

---

* One of those letters, in which Wilkes publicly addressed Horne Tooke, has the following passage; " Will you call an Italian gentleman now in town, your confidant during your whole residence at *Genoa*, to testify the morality of your conduct in Italy ? "

† *Latin*, I suspect.

a jury,—he would frequently address them as
" his little twelvers ") defended Tooke most
admirably: nay, he showed himself not only a
great orator, but a great actor; for, on the
fifth day, when the Attorney-General, Eldon, was
addressing the jury, and was using a line of
argument which Erskine had not expected and
could not reply to (the pleading for the prisoner
being closed), I well remember how Erskine the
whole time kept turning towards the jury, and
by a series of significant looks, shrugs, and
shakings of his head, did all he could to destroy
the effect of what the Attorney-General was
saying.—After a very long speech, Eldon, with
the perspiration streaming down his face, came
into the room where the Lord Mayor was
sitting, and exclaimed, " Mr. Tooke says that
he should like to send Mr. Pitt to Botany Bay;
but it would be more merciful to make him
Attorney-General."—When Eldon was told that
the mob had *taken away* the horses from Erskine's
carriage, and drawn him home in triumph to
Sergeants' Inn, he asked " If they had ever
returned them? "

At the conclusion of the trial, a daughter of
one of the jurymen was anxious to be introduced
to Tooke; who, shaking her by the hand, said
very prettily, " I must call you sister, for you
are the daughter of one of those to whom
I owe my life."—If Tooke had been con-
victed, there is no doubt that he would have
been hanged. We lived then under a reign of
terror.

One night, after dining with him at Cline's (the surgeon), I accompanied Tooke to Brandenburgh House (the Margravine of Anspach's) to see a private play. During the performance, a person behind us said, "There's that rascal Horne Tooke." The words were uttered quite distinctly; and Tooke was so offended, that he immediately withdrew. I went home with him to his house on the Common, and slept there, after sitting up very late to listen to his delightful talk.

I often dined with Tooke at Wimbledon; and always found him most pleasant and most witty. There his friends would drop in upon him without any invitation: Colonel Bosville would come frequently, bringing with him a dinner from London,—fish, &c.—Tooke latterly used to expect two or three of his most intimate friends to dine with him every Sunday; and I once offended him a good deal by not joining his Sunday dinner-parties for several weeks.

Burdett was, of course, a great deal with Tooke. In little things, Burdett was a very inconsiderate person. One forenoon, when Tooke was extremely unwell, and a friend had sent him some fine hot-house grapes, Burdett, happening to call in, ate up every one of them.

Tooke was such a passionate admirer of Milton's prose works, that, as he assured me, he had transcribed them all in his youth.

For my own part, I like Harris's* writings

* Later Lord Malmesbury.—*Ed.*

much. But Tooke thought meanly of them: he would say, " Lord Malmesbury is as great a fool *as his father*."

He used to observe, that " though the books which you have lately read may make no strong impression on you, they nevertheless improve your mind; just as food, though we forget what it was after we have eaten it, gives strength to the body."

O, the fallibility of medical people! Both Pearson and Cline, on one occasion, informed Tooke that he could not possibly survive beyond a single day: and—he lived years!—Let me mention here what was told to me by a lady at Clifton. " In my girlhood," she said, " I had a very severe illness, during which I heard Dr. Turton declare to my mother, in the next room, that *I could not live*. I immediately called out, ' But I *will* live, Dr. Turton! ' and here I am, now sixty years old."

What strange meetings sometimes occur! Richard Sharp, when a young man, was making a tour in Scotland with a friend. They arrived one night at Glencoe, and could get no lodgings at the inn; but they were told by the landlord that there lived in the neighbourhood a " laird " who was always ready to show kindness to strangers, and who would doubtless receive them into his house. Thither they went, and were treated with the greatest hospitality. In the course of conversation, the " laird " mentioned

Newfoundland as a place familiar to him.
" Have you been there? " asked Sharp. " Yes,"
he replied, " I spent some time there, when I
was in the army "; and he went on to say that,
while there, he enjoyed the society of the dearest
friend he had ever had, a gentleman named
Sharp. " Sir, I am the son of that very gentleman." The " laird " threw his arms round
Sharp's neck, and embraced him with a flood
of tears.

Sharp's little volume of *Letters and Essays* is
hardly equal to his reputation. He had given
great attention to metaphysics, and intended to
publish a work on that subject, the result of
much thought and reading. One day, as we
were walking together near Ulswater, I put some
metaphysical question to him, when he stopped
me short at once by saying, " There are only
two men* in England with whom I ever talk on
metaphysics." This was not very flattering to
me; and it so offended my sister, that she said
I ought immediately to have ordered a post-
chaise, and left him there.

I have always understood that the oration of
Pericles in Smith's *Thucydides* was translated by
Lord Chatham.

Vernon was the person who invented the
story about the lady being pulverised in India

* Meaning, I believe, Mackintosh and Bobus Smith.

by a *coup de soleil*:—when he was dining there with a Hindoo, one of his host's wives was suddenly reduced to ashes; upon which, the Hindoo *rang the bell*, and said to the attendant who answered it, "Bring fresh glasses, and sweep up your mistress."

Another of his stories was this. He happened to be shooting hyenas near Carthage, when he stumbled, and fell down an abyss of many fathoms' depth. He was surprised, however, to find himself unhurt; for he lighted as if on a feather-bed. Presently he perceived that he was gently moved upwards; and, having by degrees reached the mouth of the abyss, he again stood safe on *terra firma*. He had fallen upon an immense mass of bats, which, disturbed from their slumbers, had risen out of the abyss and brought him up with them.

I knew Joseph Warton well. When Matthias attacked him in *The Pursuits of Literature* for reprinting some loose things* in his edition of Pope, Joseph wrote a letter to me, in which he called Matthias "his *pious* critic,"—rather an odd expression to come from a clergyman.—He certainly ought not to have given that letter of Lord Cobham.†

---

* The *Imitation of the Second Satire of the First Book of Horace*, and the chapter of "The Double Mistress," in the *Memoirs of Scriblerus:* Matthias also objected to "a few trumpery, vulgar copies of verses which disgrace the pages."

† See J. Warton's *Life of Pope*, p. li. The letter had been previously printed,—in the dullest of all biographies, Ruffhead's *Life of Pope*, p. 276.

I never saw Thomas Warton. I once called at the house of Robinson the bookseller for Dr. Kippis, who used to introduce me to many literary parties, and who that evening was to take me to the Society of Antiquaries. He said, " Tom Warton is up stairs." How I now wish that I had gone up and seen him! His little poem, *The Suicide*, is a favourite of mine.—Nor did I ever see Gibbon, or Cowper, or Horace Walpole: and it is truly provoking to reflect that I *might* have seen them!

There is no doubt that Matthias wrote *The Pursuits of Literature;* and a dull poem it is, though the notes are rather piquant.

Gilbert Wakefield used to say, he was certain that Rennell and Glynn assisted Matthias in it; and Wakefield was well acquainted with all the three.

Steevens once said to Matthias, " Well, sir, since you deny the authorship of *The Pursuits of Literature*, I need have no hesitation in declaring to you that the person who wrote it is a liar and a blackguard."

In one of the notes was a statement that Beloe had received help from Porson in translating Alciphron. Porson accordingly went to Beloe,* and said, " As you know that I did *not* help you, pray, write to Matthias and desire

* The Revd. William Beloe, author of *The Sexagenarian, or Recollections of a Literary Life*, published anonymously in 1817, and characterised by Byron, in a letter to Murray, as " very amusing." A large part of the book is devoted to anecdotes of Porson.—*Ed*.

him to alter that note." In a subsequent edition the note was altered.

One day I asked Matthias if he wrote *The Pursuits of Literature;* and he answered, " My dear friend, can you suppose that I am the author of that poem, when there is no mention made in it of yourself? " Some time after, I happened to call on Lord Besborough, who told me, that, as he was illustrating *The Pursuits of Literature* with portraits, he wanted to get one of me. " Why," exclaimed I, " there is no mention in it of *me!* " He then turned to the note where I am spoken of as the banker who " dreams on Parnassus."*

What popularity Cowper's *Task* enjoyed! Johnson, the publisher, told me that, in consequence of the great number of copies which had been sold, he made a handsome present to the author.

In order to attain general popularity, a poem must have (what it is creditable to our countrymen that they look for) a strong religious tendency, and must treat of subjects which require no previous knowledge in the readers. Cowper's poems are of that description.

---

* " Let me present a short passage from a Letter to Mr. Pitt on the occasion of the Triple Assessment. ' Things, sir, are now changed. Time was, when bankers were as stupid as their guineas could make them; they were neither orators, nor painters, nor poets. But *now* Mr. Dent has a speech and *a bitch* at your service; Sir Robert has his pencil and canvas; and Mr. Rogers dreams on Parnassus; and, if I am rightly informed, there is a great demand among his brethren for *The Pleasures of Memory*.' " P. 360, ed. 1808.

Here are two fine lines in Cowper's *Task;*[*]

> " Knowledge is proud that he has learn'd so
>   much;
> Wisdom is humble that he knows no more."

Sometimes in his rhymed poetry the verses run with all the ease of prose: for instance,—

> " The path of sorrow, and that path alone,
>   Leads to the land where sorrow is
>   unknown."[†]

Cumberland[‡] was a most agreeable companion, and a very entertaining converser. His theatrical anecdotes were related with infinite spirit and humour: his description of Mrs. Siddons coming off the stage in the full flush of triumph, and walking up to the mirror in the green-room to survey herself, was admirable. He said that the three finest pieces of acting which he had ever witnessed, were Garrick's Lear, Henderson's Falstaff, and Cooke's Iago.

When Cumberland was composing any work, he never shut himself up in his study: he always wrote in the room where his family sat, and did not feel the least disturbed by the noise of his children at play beside him.

[*] Book vi.

[†] *An Epistle to an afflicted Protestant Lady in France.*

[‡] Richard Cumberland (1732–1811), the dramatist, original of Sheridan's *Sir Fretful Plagiary.—Ed.*

Lord Holland and Lord Lansdowne having expressed a wish to be introduced to Cumberland, I invited all the three to dine with me. It happened, however, that the two lords paid little or no attention to Cumberland (though he said several very good things),—scarcely speaking to him the whole time: something had occurred in the House which occupied all their thoughts; and they retired to a window, and discussed it.

Mitford, the historian of Greece, possessed, besides his learning, a wonderful variety of accomplishments. I always felt the highest respect for him. When, not long before his death, I used to meet him in the street, bent almost double, and carrying a long staff in his hand, he reminded me of a venerable pilgrim just come from Jerusalem.—His account of the Homeric age,—of the Sicilian cities,—and several other parts of his History, are very pleasing.

Lane made a large fortune by the immense quantity of trashy novels which he sent forth from his Minerva-press. I perfectly well remember the splendid carriage in which he used to ride, and his footmen with their cockades and gold-headed canes.

Now-a-days, as soon as a novel has had its run, and is beginning to be forgotten, out comes an edition of it as a " standard novel! "*

* An allusion to Bentley's *Standard Novels* series.—*Ed.*

One afternoon, at court, I was standing beside two intimate acquaintances of mine, an old nobleman and a middle-aged lady of rank, when the former remarked to the latter that he thought a certain young lady near us was uncommonly beautiful. The middle-aged lady replied, " I cannot see any particular beauty in her."—" Ah, madam," he rejoined, " to us old men youth always appears beautiful! " (a speech with which Wordsworth, when I repeated it to him, was greatly struck).—The fact is, till we are about to leave the world, we do not perceive how much it contains to excite our interest and admiration: the sunsets appear to me far lovelier now than they were in other years; and the bee upon the flower is now an object of curiosity to me, which it was not in my early days.

With the exception of some good lines, such as,—

" Hell in his heart, and Tyburn in his face,"*

Churchill's poetry is, to my thinking, but mediocre; and for such poetry I have little toleration; though perhaps, when I recollect my own writings, I ought not to make the remark.

I am not sure that I do not prefer Wolcot (Peter Pindar) to Churchill.—Wolcot's *Gipsy*† is very neat.

* *The Author*.
† Not inserted in Wolcot's collected *Works*.

[" A wandering gipsy, sirs, am I,
  From Norwood, where we oft complain,
With many a tear and many a sigh,
  Of blustering winds and rushing rain.

No costly rooms or gay attire
  Within our humble shed appear;
No beds of down, or blazing fire,
  At night our shivering limbs to cheer.

Alas, no friend comes near our cot!
  The redbreasts only find the way,
Who give their all, a simple note,
  At peep of morn and parting day.

But *fortunes* here I come to tell,—
  Then yield me, gentle sir, your hand:—
Within these lines what thousands
    dwell,—
  And, bless me, what a heap of land!

It surely, sir, must pleasing be
  To hold such wealth in every line:
Try, pray, now try, if you can see
  A little treasure lodg'd in mine."]

And there can hardly be a better line of its
kind than this,—

  " Kill half a cow, and turn the rest to grass."*

* *Complimentary Epistle to James Boswell, Esq.*

99

In company with my sister, I paid a visit to Gilbert Wakefield when he was in Dorchester Gaol.* His confinement was made as pleasant to him as possible; for he had nearly an acre of ground to walk about in. But, still, the sentence passed upon him was infamous: what rulers we had in those days!

At a splendid party given by Lord Hampden to the Prince of Wales, &c., I saw Lady Hamilton go through all those " attitudes " which have been engraved; and her performance was very beautiful indeed. Her husband, Sir William, was present.

Lord Nelson was a remarkably kind-hearted man. I have seen him spin a teetotum with his *one* hand, a whole evening, for the amusement of some children. I heard him once during dinner utter many bitter complaints (which Lady Hamilton vainly attempted to check) of the way he had been treated at court that forenoon: the Queen had not condescended to take the slightest notice of him. In truth, Nelson was hated at court; they were jealous of his fame.

There was something very charming in Lady Hamilton's openness of manner. She showed me the neckcloth which Nelson had on when he died: of course, I could not help looking at it with extreme interest; and she threw her

* Imprisoned for writing a pamphlet against William Pitt's new Income Tax.—*Ed*.

arms round my neck and kissed me.—She was latterly in great want; and Lord Stowell never rested till he procured for her a small pension from government.

Parson Este was well acquainted with Mrs. Robinson (the once-celebrated *Perdita*), and said that Fox had the greatest difficulty in persuading the Prince of Wales to lend her some assistance when, towards the close of life, she was in very straitened circumstances. Este saw her funeral, which was attended by a single mourning coach.*

A person once asserted that in a particular country the bees were as large as sheep. He was asked " How big, then, are the hives? "— " Oh," he replied, " the usual size."

I knew Jane Duchess of Gordon intimately, and many pleasant hours have I passed in her society. She used to say, " I have been acquainted with David Hume and William Pitt, and therefore I am not afraid to converse with any body."

* Poor Perdita had some poetic talent: and it was acknowledged by Coleridge, whose lines to her, " As late on Skiddaw's mount I lay supine," &c., are not to be found in the recent collections of his poems. See, at p. xlviii. of the Tributary Poems prefixed to *Mrs. Robinson's Poetical Works*, 3 vols., " *A Stranger Minstrel. By S. T. Coleridge, Esq., written a few weeks before her death*," and dated " Nov. 1800."

The Duchess told the following anecdote to
Lord Stowell, who told it to Lord Dunmore,
who told it to me. "The son of Lord Corn-
wallis [Lord Brome] fell in love with my daughter
Louisa; and she liked him much. They were
to be married; but the intended match was
broken off by Lord C., whose only objection to
it sprung from his belief that there was madness
in my husband's family. Upon this I contrived
to have a *tête-à-tête* with Lord C., and said to
him, ' I know your reason for disapproving of
your son's marriage with my daughter: now, I
will tell you one thing plainly,—*there is not a drop
of the Gordon blood in Louisa's body.*' With this
statement Lord C. was quite satisfied, and the
marriage took place." The Duchess prided
herself greatly on the success of this manœuvre,
though it had forced her to slander her own
character so cruelly and so unjustly! In fact,
manœuvring was her delight.

One morning I was about to mount my horse
to ride into London to the banking-house, when,
to my astonishment, I read in the newspapers
that a summons had been issued to bring me
before the Privy-Council. I immediately proceeded to Downing Street, and asked to see Mr.
Dundas. I was admitted; and I told him that
I had come to inquire the cause of the summons
which I had seen announced in the newspapers.
He said, " Have you a carriage here? " I
replied, " A hackney-coach." Into it we got;

and there was I sitting familiarly with Dundas, whom I had never before set eyes on. We drove to the Home-Office; and I learned that I had been summoned to give evidence in the case of William Stone, accused of high treason. —Long before this, I had met Stone in the Strand, when he told me, among other things, that a person had arrived here from France to gather the sentiments of the people of England concerning a French invasion; and that he (Stone) would call upon me and read to me a paper on that subject. I said, " You will infect me with the plague "; and we parted. In the course of a few days he *did* call with the paper. —After the Government had laid hold of Stone, he mentioned his intercourse with me; and hence my summons. When his trial took place, I was examined by the Attorney-General, and cross-examined by Erskine. For some time before the trial I could scarcely get a wink of sleep: the thoughts of my appearance at it made me miserable.

[Extract from *The Trial of William Stone, for High Treason, at the Bar of the Court of King's Bench, on Thursday the Twenty-eighth and Friday the Twenty-ninth of January* 1796. *Taken in shorthand by Joseph Gurney*, 1796.

" *Samuel Rogers, Esq.* (sworn.)

Examined by *Mr. Attorney-General.*

Q. You know Mr. William Stone?
A. Yes.

Q. Do you know Mr. Hurford Stone?

A. I have known him many years.

Q. Do you recollect having any conversation —and if you do, be so good as to state to my Lord and the Jury, what conversation you had with Mr. William Stone relative to an invasion of this country?

A. He met me, I think it was in the month of March 1794, in the street; he stopped me to mention the receipt of a letter from his brother at Paris, on the arrival of a gentleman, who wished particularly to collect the sentiments of the people of this country with respect to a French invasion.—Our conversation went very little further, for it was in the street.

Q. Do you recollect what you said to him, if you said any thing?

A. I recollect that I rather declined the conversation.

Q. I ask you, not what you declined or did not decline, but what you said to him, if you said any thing.

A. I was in a hurry, and I believe all I said was to decline the conversation.

Q. State in what language you did decline that conversation.

A. I said that I had no wish to take any part whatever in any political transactions at that time; it was a time of general alarm, and I wished to shun even the shadow of an imputation, as I knew that when the minds of men were agitated, as I thought they then were, the most innocent intentions were liable to misconstruction.

Q. Did he inform you who the person was?

A. No, he did not; I only learned that it was a gentleman arrived from Paris; I speak from recollection.

Q. Did he inform you what gentleman he was?

A. I do not recollect that he did.

Q. Did he ever call upon you after you had declined this conversation?

A. He did call upon me a few days after; and he read to me a paper, which I understood to be written by somebody else, but I cannot say who; and which went to show, as far as I can recollect, that the English nation, however they might differ among themselves, would unite to repel an invasion.

Q. After you had declined a conversation upon this subject, from motives of discretion, Mr. Stone called upon you and showed you this paper?

A. He told me in the street he should call upon me.

Q. Had you any further conversation with him at any time upon this subject?

A. He mentioned at that time that he thought he should do his duty, if, by stating what he believed to be true, he could save the country from an invasion.

Q. Did he ever tell you where this gentleman went to afterwards?

A. I never had any further conversation with him upon the subject.

Q. He never came to consult you about what this gentleman was doing any where but in England?

A. No; I believe I never met him again.

Samuel Rogers, Esq.

Cross-examined by *Mr. Erskine*.

Q. Mr. Stone, meeting you accidentally in the street, communicated this to you?

A. In the open street.

Q. Not with any secrecy?

A. By no means.

Q. And you might have told it me, if I had happened to have met you five minutes afterwards?

A. Very likely.

Q. Have you had any acquaintance with Mr. Stone?

A. I have met him frequently for many years.

Q. What is his character with respect to loyalty to his king, and regard to his country?

A. I had always an opinion that in that respect he was a very well-meaning man."

pp. 144–6.]

I cannot relish Shakespeare's *Sonnets*. The song in *As you like it*, " Blow, blow, thou winter wind," is alone worth them all.

Do not allow yourself to be imposed upon by the authority of great names: there is not a little both in Shakespeare and in Milton that is

very far from good. The famous passage in
Hamlet, though it has passed into a sort of
proverbial expression, is downright nonsense,—

> " a custom
> More honour'd in the breach than the
> observance: "

how can a custom be honoured in the breach
of it?

In Milton's description of the lazar-house
there is a dreadful confusion of metaphor:—

> " Sight so deform what *heart of rock* could long
> *Dry-ey'd* behold? "*

I once observed this to Coleridge, who told
Wordsworth that he could not sleep all the
next night for thinking of it.

Some speeches in *Paradise Lost* have as much
dramatic force as any thing in Shakespeare;
for instance,—

> " Know ye not, then, said Satan fill'd with
>   scorn,
> Know ye not me? Ye knew me once no
>   mate
> For you, there sitting where ye durst not
>   soar," &c.†

It is remarkable that no poet before Shakespeare ever introduced a person *walking in sleep*.

* *Par. Lost*, b. xi. 494.
† *Par. Lost*, b. iv. 827.

I believe there is no allusion to such a circumstance in any of the Greek or Latin poets.—What a play that is! was there ever such a ghost?—" the table's full! " I never missed going to see it, when Kemble and Mrs. Siddons played Macbeth and Lady Macbeth: their noble acting, and Locke's fine music, made it a delightful treat.

If you wish to have your works *coldly* reviewed, get your intimate friend to write an article on them. I know this by experience.—Ward (Lord Dudley) " cut up " my *Columbus* in *The Quarterly:* but he afterwards repented of it, and apologised to me.*

* The No. of *The Quarterly* (see vol. ix. 207) which contained the critique in question had just appeared, when Mr. Rogers, who had not yet seen it, called on Lord Grosvenor, and found Gifford sitting with him. Between Mr. Rogers and Gifford there was little cordiality; but on that occasion they chatted together in a very friendly manner. After Mr. Rogers had left the room, Gifford said to Lord Grosvenor with a smile, " Do you think he has seen the last *Quarterly?* "

Mr. Rogers took his revenge for that critique by frequently repeating the following epigram, which has been erroneously attributed to others, but which, as Mr. Rogers told me, *he himself wrote, with some little assistance from Richard Sharp:*

" Ward has no heart, they say; but I deny it;—
He has a heart, and gets his speeches by it."

Columbus was first printed in a thin quarto, for private circulation, 1810. When Ward reviewed it in 1813, as forming a portion of Mr. Rogers's collected poems, it had been greatly enlarged.

Another article in *The Quarterly* gave considerable annoyance to Mr. Rogers,—the critique by George Ellis on Byron's *Corsair* and *Lara* (vol. xi. 428), in which Mr. Rogers's *Jacqueline* (originally appended to *Lara*) is only mentioned as " the highly refined, but somewhat insipid, pastoral tale of Jacqueline."—When Mr. Rogers was at Brighton in 1851, Lady Byron told him that her husband, on
(*continued on next page*)

I have seen Howard the philanthropist more than once: he was a remarkably mild-looking man. His books,—*The State of the Prisons in England and Wales*, &c., and *An Account of the principal Lazarettos in Europe*, &c.,—are excellently written. It is not generally known that he had considerable assistance from Dr. Price in composing them.*

Sir Henry Englefield had a fancy (which some greater men have had) that there was about his person a natural odour of roses and violets. Lady Grenville, hearing of this, and loving a joke, exclaimed, one day when Sir Henry was present, " Bless me, what a smell of violets! "— " Yes," said he with great simplicity; " it comes from me."

We have in England the finest series of pictures and the finest of sculptures in the

(continued from previous page)
reading Ellis's critique, had said, " The man's a fool. *Jacqueline* is as superior to *Lara* as Rogers is to me." Who will believe that Byron said this sincerely? Yet *Jacqueline* is undoubtedly a beautiful little poem.

* " As I thought it right to mention Mr. Howard's literary deficiencies, it is become necessary to inform the public of the manner in which his works were composed. On his return from his tours he took all his memorandum-books to an old retired friend of his, who assisted him in methodising them, and copied out the whole matter in correct language. They were then put into the hands of Dr. Price, from whom they underwent a revision, and received occasionally considerable alterations." Aikin's *View of the Character and Public Services of the late John Howard*, p. 64.

world,—I mean, the Cartoons of Raphael and the Elgin Marbles.

Our National Gallery is superior to any private collection of pictures in Italy,—superior, for instance, to the Doria and Borghese collections, which contain several very indifferent things.

Perhaps the choicest private collection in this country is that at Panshanger (Earl Cowper's): it is small, but admirable; what Raphaels, what Andrea del Sartos, what Claudes!

In former days Cuyp's pictures were comparatively little valued: he was the first artist who painted *light*, and therefore he was not understood. Sir William Beechy was at a picture-sale with Wilson, when one of Cuyp's pieces was knocked down for a trifling sum. " Well," said Wilson, " the day *will* come when both Cuyp's works and my own will bring the prices which they ought to bring."

Look at this engraving by Marc Antonio after Raphael,—Michael treading upon Satan, and note its superiority to Guido's picture on the same subject.   In the latter, the countenance of Michael expresses triumph alone; in the former, it expresses triumph mingled with pity for a fallen brother-angel.

This Last Supper by Raphael [Marc Antonio's engraving] is, I think, in all respects superior to that by Lionardo. The apostle on the right hand of Christ strikingly displays his indignation against the betrayer of his Lord by grasping the table-knife.

Never in any picture did I see such a figure as this,—I mean, a figure so completely floating on the air [the Angel holding the wreath in Marc Antonio's engraving, after Raphael, of the martyrdom of St. Felicita].

Sir Thomas Lawrence used to say, that among painters there were three pre-eminent for *invention*,—Giorgione, Rembrandt, and Rubens; and perhaps he was right.

Sir Thomas Lawrence has painted several very pleasing pictures of children; but generally his men are effeminate, and his women meretricious.—Of his early portraits Sir Joshua Reynolds said, "This young man has a great deal of talent; but there is an affectation in his style which he will never entirely shake off."

We have now in England a greater number of tolerably good painters than ever existed here together at any former period: but, alas, we have no Hogarth, and no Reynolds!

I must not, however, forget that we have Turner,—a man of first-rate genius in his line. There is in some of his pictures a grandeur which neither Claude nor Poussin could give to theirs.

Turner thinks that Rubens's landscapes are deficient in *nature*. I differ from him. Indeed, *there** is a proof that he is mistaken; look at that forest-scene by Rubens; the foreground of it is truth itself.

The Art Union is a perfect curse: it buys and engraves very inferior pictures, and consequently encourages mediocrity of talent; it makes young men, who have no genius, abandon the desk and counter, and set up for painters.

The public gave little encouragement to Flaxman and Banks, but showered its patronage on two much inferior sculptors, Bacon and Chantrey.

As to Flaxman, the greatest sculptor of his day,—the neglect which *he* experienced is something inconceivable. Canova, who was well acquainted with his exquisite illustrations of Dante, &c., could hardly believe that a man of such genius was not an object of admiration among his countrymen; and, in allusion to their insensibility to Flaxman's merits and to their patronage of inferior artists, he said to some of the English at Rome, " *You* see with your ears! "

Chantrey began his career by being a carver in wood. The ornaments on that mahogany sideboard, and on that stand [in Mr. Rogers's

* *i.e.* on the wall of Mr. Rogers's dining-room.

dining-room], were carved by him. [Subsequently, when a gentleman informed Mr. Rogers that the truth of this last statement had been questioned, he entered into the following particulars.—Chantrey said to me one day, " Do you recollect that, about twenty-five years ago, a journeyman came to your house, from the woodcarver employed by you and Mr. Hope, to talk about these ornaments, and that you gave him a drawing to execute them by? " I replied that I recollected it perfectly. " Well," continued Chantrey, " *I* was that journeyman."] When he was at Rome in the height of his celebrity, he injured himself not a little by talking with contempt* of the finest statues of antiquity.—Jackson (the painter) told me that he and Chantrey went into the studio of Dannecker the sculptor, who happened to be from home. There was an unfinished bust in the room; and Chantrey, taking up a chisel, proceeded to work upon it. One of the assistants immediately rushed forwards, in great alarm, to stop him; but no sooner had Chantrey given a blow on the chisel, than the man exclaimed, with a knowing look, " Ha! ha! "—as much as to say, " I see that you perfectly understand what you are about."—Chantrey practised portrait-painting both at Sheffield and after he came to London. It was in allusion to him

---

* Mr. Rogers, I apprehend, was mistaken on this point. From Jones's *Life of Chantrey*, p. 26, it appears that Chantrey did not admire those statues so much as they are generally admired, and therefore was unwilling to give his opinion on them; but that he never spoke of them " with contempt."

that Lawrence said, "A broken-down painter will make a very good sculptor."

Ottley's* knowledge of painting was astonishing. Showing him a picture which I had just received from Italy, I said, "Whose work do you suppose it to be?" After looking at it attentively, he replied, "It is the work of Lorenzo di Credi" (by whom I already knew that it was painted).—"How," I asked, "could you discover it to be from Lorenzo's pencil? have you ever before now seen any of his pieces?" "Never," he answered; "but I am familiar with the description of his style as given by Vasari and others."

I regret that so little of Curran's brilliant talk has been preserved. How much of it Tom Moore could record, if he would only take the trouble!

I once dined with Curran in the public room of the chief inn at Greenwich, when he talked a great deal, and, as usual, with considerable exaggeration. Speaking of something which he would *not* do on any inducement, he exclaimed vehemently, "I had rather be hanged upon twenty gibbets."—"Don't you think, sir, that *one* would be enough for you?" said a girl, a stranger, who was sitting at the table next to us.

* W. Y. Ottley (1771–1836), the connoisseur and art-collector.—*Ed.*

I wish you could have seen Curran's face. He was absolutely confounded,—struck dumb.

Very few persons know that the poem called *Ulm and Trafalgar** was written by Canning. He composed it (as George Ellis told me) in about two days, while he walked up and down the room. Indeed, very few persons know that such a poem exists.

After Legge was appointed Bishop of Oxford, he had the folly to ask two wits, Canning and Frere, to be present at his first sermon. " Well," said he to Canning, " how did you like it? " " Why, I thought it rather—short."—" Oh, yes, I am aware that it was short; but I was afraid of being tedious." " You *were* tedious."

A lady having put to Canning the silly question, " Why have they made the spaces in the iron gate at Spring Gardens† so narrow? " he replied, " Oh, ma'am, because such very fat people used to go through " (a reply concerning which Tom Moore said, that " the person who does not relish it can have no perception of real wit ").

I once mentioned to Canning the anecdote,‡

* A short poem printed for Ridgeway, 1806, 4to.

† At the end of Spring Garden Passage, which opens into St. James's Park.

‡ Whence this very suspicious version of the anecdote was derived I cannot learn. In a Ms. note of Cole it is given as follows: " One of their tricks was, knowing that Mr. Gray had [having ?] a dread of fire, had rope-ladders in his chamber; they alarmed him in the middle of the night with the cry of fire, in hope of seeing him make use of them from his window, in the middle story of the new building." —Mitford's *Gray*, i. cviii. It was in consequence of these " tricks " that Gray removed from Peter House to Pembroke Hall.

that, while Gray was at Peter House, Cambridge, some young men of the college having learned that he had a fire-escape in his rooms, alarmed him in the middle of the night by a cry of " fire," —and that presently Gray descended from the window by a ladder of ropes, and tumbled into a tub of water, which the rogues had placed there;—upon which, Canning added, that " they had made a mistake in calling out ' fire,' when they meant to cry ' water.' "

Canning said that a man who could talk of liking *dry* champagne would not scruple to say any thing.

The Duke of York told me that Dr. Cyril Jackson* most conscientiously did his duty as tutor to him and his brother, the Prince of Wales. " Jackson," said the Duke, " used to have a silver pencil-case in his hand while we were at our lessons; and he has frequently given us such knocks with it upon our foreheads, that the blood followed them."

I have often heard the Duke relate how he and his brother George, when young men, were robbed by footpads on Hay Hill. They had dined that day at Devonshire House, had then gone home to lay aside their court-dresses, and afterwards proceeded to a house of a certain description in the neighbourhood of Berkeley Square. They were returning from it in a hackney-coach, late at night, when some footpads

* One time Dean of Christ Church, Oxford.—*Ed.*

stopped them on Hay Hill, and carried off their purses, watches, &c.

In his earlier days the Duke of York was most exact in paying all his debts of honour. One night at Brookes's, while he was playing cards, he said to Lord Thanet, who was about to go home to bed, " Lord Thanet, is our betting still to continue? " " Yes, sir, certainly," was the reply: and next morning Lord Thanet found 1500*l.* left for him at Brookes's by the Duke. But gradually he became less particular in such matters; and at last he would quietly pocket the winnings of the night from Lord Robert Spencer, though he owed Lord Robert about five thousand pounds.

I have several times stayed at Oatlands with the Duke and Duchess of York—both of them most amiable and agreeable persons. We were generally a company of about fifteen; and our being invited to remain there " another day " sometimes depended on the ability of our royal host and hostess to raise sufficient money for our entertainment. We used to have all sorts of ridiculous " fun " as we roamed about the grounds. The Duchess kept (besides a number of dogs, for which there was a regular burial-place) a collection of monkeys, each of which had its own pole with a house at top. One of the visitors (whose name I forget) would single out a particular monkey, and play to it on the fiddle with such fury and perseverance, that the poor animal, half-distracted, would at last take refuge in the arms of Lord Alvanley.—Monk

Lewis was a great favourite at Oatlands. One day after dinner, as the Duchess was leaving the room, she whispered something into Lewis's ear. He was much affected, his eyes filling with tears. We asked what was the matter. " Oh," replied Lewis, " the Duchess spoke so *very* kindly to me! " —" My dear fellow," said Colonel Armstrong,* " pray don't cry; I daresay she didn't mean it."

I was in the pit of the Opera with Crabbe the poet when the Duchess of York beckoned to me, and I went into her box. There was no one with her except a lady, whom I did not know; and supposing that she was only one of the Duchess's attendants, I talked very unguardedly about the Duke of Kent. Now, the lady was the Duchess of Gloucester, who took great offence at what I said, and has never forgiven me for it. The Duchess of York told me afterwards that she sat in perfect misery, expecting that, when I had done with the Duke of Kent, I should fall upon the Duke of Gloucester.

In Monk Lewis's writings there is a deal of bad taste; but still he was a man of genius. I'll tell you two stories which he was very fond of repeating (and which Windham used to like). The first is:

The Skeleton in the Church-porch.
Some travellers were supping at an inn in

* Query about this name ? Sometimes, while telling the story, Mr. Rogers would say, " I think it was Colonel Armstrong."

Germany, and sent for the landlord to give him a glass of wine. In the course of conversation the landlord remarked that a certain person whom they happened to speak of, was as obstinate as the Skeleton in the Church-porch. " What is that? " they inquired. The landlord said that he alluded to a skeleton which it was impossible to keep under ground; that he had twice or thrice assisted in laying it in the charnel, but that always, the day after it had been buried, it was found lying in the church-porch. The travellers were greatly struck by this account; and they expressed an eager desire to see the refractory skeleton. At last, a young serving-woman coming into the room, they asked her if she, for a reward, would go to the church-porch and bring the skeleton to them. She at first refused to do so; but eventually the travellers offered a sum of money which she could not resist. Be it particularly observed that the young woman was then *big with child*. Well, off she set to the church; and having found the skeleton in its usual place, she brought it to the inn on her back, and laid it upon the table before the travellers. They had no sooner looked at it than they wished it gone; and they prevailed on the young woman, for another sum of money, to carry it again to the church-porch. When she arrived there, she set it down; and turning away, she was proceeding quickly along the path which led from the church, and which was seen stretching out before her in the clear moonlight, when suddenly she felt the skeleton leap upon her back. She tried to shake it off; but in vain. She then fell on her knees, and said her prayers. The skeleton relaxed its hold; and she again rushed down the path, when, as before, the skeleton leapt upon her back. " I will never quit you," it said, " till you descend into the charnel, and obtain forgiveness for the skeleton that lies in the church-porch." She paused a moment; then summoning up her courage, she replied that she would do so. The skeleton dropped off. Down she went into the charnel; and, after groping about for some time, she perceived the pale figure of a lady, sitting by a lamp and reading. She advanced towards the figure, and, kneeling, said, " I ask forgiveness for the skeleton that lies in the church-porch." The lady read on without looking at her. Again she repeated her supplication, but still the lady read on, regardless of it. The young woman then ascended from the charnel, and was running down the path when the skeleton once more arrested her progress. " I will never quit you," it said, " till you obtain forgiveness for the skeleton that lies in the church-porch: go again into the charnel, and ask it." Again the young woman descended, and, advancing to the lady, sunk upon her knees, and cried, " I come a second time to ask forgiveness for the skeleton that lies in the church-porch. Oh, grant that forgiveness! the skeleton implores it! I implore it! *the babe that I bear in my womb implores it also!* " The lady turned her head towards the speaker, gave a faint smile, and disappeared. On coming up from the charnel, the young woman found the skeleton standing erect in the porch. "I am now here," it said, "not to trouble you, but to thank you: you have at length procured me rest in the grave. I was betrothed to the lady whom you saw in the charnel; and I basely deserted her for another. I stood at the altar, about to be married to my second love, when suddenly the lady rushed into the church, and having stabbed herself with a dagger, said to me, as she was expiring, "You shall never have rest in the grave,—no, never, *till the babe unborn shall ask forgiveness for you.*" The skeleton rewarded the good offices of the young woman by discovering to her the place where a heap of treasure was concealed.

The second story is:

Lord Howth's Rat.

Tom Sheridan was shooting on the moors in Ireland, and lost his dog. A day or two after, it made its appearance, following an Irish labourer. It was restored to Sheridan, who remarked to the labourer that "the dog seemed very familiar with him." The answer was, "Yes, it follows me, as the rat did Lord Howth." An inquiry about this rat drew forth what is now to be told.—Lord Howth, having dissipated his property, retired in very low spirits to a lonely chateau on the sea-coast. One stormy

night a vessel was seen to go down; and next
morning a raft was beheld floating towards the
shore. As it approached, the bystanders were
surprised to find that it was guided by a lady,
who presently stepped upon the beach. She
was exquisitely beautiful; but they were unable
to discover who or what she was, for she spoke
in an unknown tongue. Lord Howth was
struck with great pity for this fair stranger, and
conducted her to his chateau. There she remained a considerable time, when he became
violently enamoured of her, and at last asked
her to become his wife. She (having now learned
the English language) thanked him for the
honour he had intended her; but declared in
the most positive terms that she could never be
his. She then earnestly advised him to marry
a certain lady of a neighbouring county. He
followed her advice; paid his addresses to the
lady, and was accepted. Before the marriage,
the beautiful stranger took a ribbon from her
hair, and binding it round the wrist of Lord
Howth, said, " Your happiness depends on your
never parting with this ribbon." He assured
her that it should remain constantly on his
wrist. She then disappeared, and was never
seen again. The marriage took place. The
ribbon was a matter of much wonder and
curiosity to the bride; and one night, while
Lord Howth was asleep, she removed it from
his wrist, and carried it to the fire, that she
might read the characters inscribed upon it.
Accidentally she let the flame reach it, and it

was consumed. Some time after, Lord Howth was giving a grand banquet in his hall, when the company were suddenly disturbed by the barking of dogs. This, the servants said, was occasioned by a rat which the dogs were pursuing. Presently the rat, followed by the dogs, entered the hall. It mounted on the table, and running up to Lord Howth, stared at him earnestly with its bright black eyes. He saved its life; and from that moment it never quitted him: wherever he was, alone or with his friends, there was the rat. At last the society of the rat became very disagreeable to Lord Howth; and his brother urged him to leave Ireland for a time, that he might get rid of it. He did so, and proceeded to Marseilles, accompanied by his brother. They had just arrived at that place, and were sitting in the room of an hotel, when the door opened, and in came the rat. It was dripping wet, and went straight to the fire to dry itself. Lord Howth's brother, greatly enraged at the intrusion, seized the poker, and dashed out its brains. "You have murdered me," cried Lord Howth, and instantly expired.

Grattan's aunt was intimate with Swift's Stella (Mrs. Johnson), who would sometimes sleep with her in the same bed, and pass the whole night in tears. Stella was not handsome.

At one of Lady Crewe's dinner-parties, Grattan, after talking very delightfully for some time, all at once seemed disconcerted, and sunk into silence. I asked his daughter, who was sitting next to me, the reason of this. "Oh," she replied, " he has just found out that he has come here in his powdering-coat."

Grattan said that Malone went about, looking, through strongly-magnifying spectacles, for pieces of straw and bits of broken glass.

He declared that the two greatest men of modern times were William the Third and Washington.

"Three persons," said Grattan, "are considered as having the best claim to the authorship of *Junius's Letters*,—Gibbon, Hamilton, and Burke. Gibbon is out of the question. I do not believe that they were Hamilton's; because a man, who was willing to be known as the author of a bad piece, would hardly have failed to acknowledge that he had written an excellent book. I incline to think that Burke was Junius."

"Burke," observed Grattan, "became at last such an enthusiastic admirer of kingly power, that he could not have slept comfortably on his pillow, if he had not thought that the king had a right to carry it off from under his head."

"Do you ever say your prayers?" asked Plunkett of Grattan. "No, never."—"What, never! neither night nor morning?" "Never: but I have aspirations all day long."

"What you have just mentioned," said one of Grattan's friends to him, "is a profound secret: where *could* you have heard it?"

Grattan replied, " Where secrets are kept,—in the street."

You remember the passage in my *Human Life?*—

> " A walk in spring—Grattan, like those with thee
> By the heath-side (who had not envied me?),
> When the sweet limes, so full of bees in June,
> Led us to meet beneath their boughs at noon;
> And thou didst say which of the great and wise,
> Could they but hear and at thy bidding rise,
> Thou wouldst call up and question."

I allude to some lime-trees near Tunbridge Wells. Grattan would say to me, " Come, Rogers, let's take a walk among the lime-trees, and hear those great senators, the bees "; and, while we were listening to their buzzing and humming, he would exclaim, " Now they are holding a committee," &c. &c. He would say, too, " Were I a necromancer, I should like to call up Scipio Africanus: he was not so skilful a captain as Hannibal; but he was a greater and more virtuous man. And I should like to talk to Julius Cæsar on several points of his history,—on one particularly (though I would not press the subject, if disagreeable to him);—I should wish to know what part he took during Catiline's conspiracy."—" Should you like to call up Cleopatra? " I asked. " No," replied Grattan, " not Cleopatra: she would tell me nothing but lies; and her beauty would make me sad."*— Grattan was so fond of walking with me, that Mrs. Grattan once said to him rather angrily, " You'll be taken for Mr. Rogers's shadow."

" How I should like," said Grattan one day to me, " to spend my whole life in a small neat cottage! I could be content with very little; I should need only cold meat, and bread, and beer,—*and plenty of claret.*"

I once said to Grattan, " If you were now only twenty years old, and Cook were about to set sail round the world, should you like to accompany him? " He answered, " I have no wish to see such countries as he saw: I should like to see Rome, Athens, and some parts of Asia; but little besides."

He declared that he had rather be shot than go up in a balloon.

Grattan's uncle, Dean Marlay, gave the nicest little dinners and kept the best company in Dublin: his parties were delightful. At that time he had about four hundred a year. Afterwards, when he succeeded to an estate and was made a Bishop, he gave great dinners chiefly to people of rank and fashion (foolish men and foolish women); and his parties lost all their charm.

He had a good deal of the humour of Swift.

* The very reverse of the effect which the beauty of the little cottage-girl produced on Wordsworth—" Her beauty made me *glad.*" *We are Seven.* Speaking to me of the poem just cited, Wordsworth said, " It is founded on fact. I met a little girl near Goderich Castle, who, though some of her brothers and sisters were dead, *would* talk of them in the present tense. I wrote that poem backward,—that is, I began with the last stanza."

Once, when the footman was out of the way, he ordered the coachman to fetch some water from the well. To this the coachman objected, that *his* business was to *drive*, not to run on errands. " Well, then," said Marlay, " bring out the coach and four, set the pitcher inside, and *drive* to the well; "—a service which was several times repeated, to the great amusement of the village.

Places are given away by Government as often for the sake of silencing animosity as in the hope of assistance from the parties benefited.

The French Revolution was the greatest event in Europe since the irruption of the Goths.

The most beautiful and magnificent view on the face of the earth is the prospect of Mont Blanc from the Jura Mountains.

Archibald Hamilton, afterwards Duke of Hamilton, (as his daughter, Lady Dunmore, told me) advertised for " a Hermit " as an ornament to his pleasure-grounds; and it was stipulated that the said Hermit should have his beard shaved but once a year, and that only partially.

A friend, calling on him one forenoon, asked if it was true that he kept a young tame tiger. He immediately slapped his thighs, and uttered a sort of whistle; and forth crept the long-backed animal from under the sofa. The visitor soon retreated.

Lord Shelburne could say the most provoking things, and yet appear quite unconscious of their being so. In one of his speeches, alluding to Lord Carlisle, he said, " The noble lord has written a comedy." " No, a tragedy."—" Oh, I beg pardon; *I thought it was a comedy.*"

Only look at that sunset! it is enough to make one feel devout.—I was once driving through the Park on my way to a dinner-party, when the sun was setting so beautifully that I could not resist staying to see all that I could see of it; and so I desired the coachman to drive me round and round till it was fairly set. Dinner was begun when I arrived; but that did not much matter.

Once at Thomas Grenville's house I was rapturously admiring a sunset. " Yes," he observed, " it is very *handsome*: " and some time after, when —— was admiring another sunset, he said, " Why, you are as foolish as Rogers."

When a lady, a friend of mine, was in Italy,

she went into a church, and knelt down among the crowd. An Italian woman, who was praying at some little distance, rose up, came softly to my friend, whispered in her ear, " If you continue to flirt with my husband, I'll be the death of you "; and then, as softly, returned to her genuflections. Such things cannot happen where there are pews.

I know few lines finer than the concluding stanza of *Life** by Mrs. Barbauld, who composed it when she was very old;

> " Life! we've been long together,
> Through pleasant and through cloudy weather:
> 'Tis hard to part when friends are dear;
> Perhaps 'twill cost a sigh, a tear;
> Then steal away, give little warning,
>   Choose thine own time,
> Say not Good Night, but in some brighter clime
>   Bid me Good Morning."

Sitting with Madame D'Arblay some weeks before she died, I said to her, " Do you remember those lines of Mrs. Barbauld's *Life* which I once repeated to you? " " Remember them! " she replied; " I repeat them to myself every night before I go to sleep."

* Wordsworth also thought very highly of these lines: see his *Memoirs*, ii. 222.

Strangely enough,* in spite of her correct taste, Mrs. Barbauld was quite fascinated by Darwin's *Botanic Garden* when it first appeared, and talked of it with rapture; for which I scolded her heartily.

One day, as she was going to Hampstead in the stage-coach, she had a Frenchman for her companion; and entering into conversation with him, she found that he was making an excursion to Hampstead for the express purpose of *seeing the house in the Flask Walk* where Clarissa Harlowe lodged.† What a compliment to the genius of Richardson!

A few days before his death, Bobus Smith‡ said to me, "Rogers, however we may doubt on some points, we have made up our minds on

* It is not so strange, when we recollect that *The Botanic Garden* fascinated even Cowper: see his verses to Darwin, written in conjunction with Hayley.—Wordsworth once said to me: " Darwin had not an atom of feeling: he was a mere eye-voluptuary. He has so many similes all beginning with ' So,' that I used to call *The Botanic Garden* ' so-so poetry.' "

† " The writer of these observations well remembers a Frenchman who paid a visit to Hampstead for the sole purpose of finding out the house in the *Flask-walk* where Clarissa lodged, and was surprised at the ignorance or indifference of the inhabitants on that subject. The *Flask-walk* was to him as much classic ground as the rocks of Meillerie to the admirers of Rousseau; and probably, if an English traveller were to make similar inquiries in Switzerland, he would find that the rocks of Meillerie and the *chalets* of the Valais suggested no ideas to the inhabitants but such as were connected with their dairies and their farms. A constant residence soon destroys all sensibility to objects of local enthusiasm." Mrs. Barbauld's *Life of Richardson*, p. cix.

‡ *i.e.* Robert Smith, the elder brother of Sydney, and one of the best writers of Latin verse since the days of the ancients. *Bobus* was the nickname given to him by his schoolfellows at Eton.

one,—that Christ was sent into the world commissioned by the almighty to instruct mankind." I replied, "Yes; of that I am perfectly convinced."

When I was a lad, I recollect seeing a whole cartful of young girls, in dresses of various colours, on their way to be executed at Tyburn. They had all been condemned, on one indictment, for having been concerned in (that is, perhaps, for having been spectators of) the burning of some houses during Lord George Gordon's riots. It was quite horrible.—Greville was present at one of the trials consequent on those riots, and heard several boys sentenced, to their own excessive amazement, to be hanged. " Never," said Greville with great *naïveté*, " did I see boys *cry so*."

I once observed to a friend of mine, " Why, you and Mr. —— live like two brothers." He replied, " God forbid! " And it must be confessed that most of the " misunderstandings " which we hear of, exist between brothers and sisters. These " misunderstandings " often arise from the eminence acquired by some one member of a family, which the others cannot endure.

In my youth, just as I was beginning to be a little known, I felt much gratified by an invitation to breakfast with Townley, the statue collector; and one night, at home, I mentioned the invitation. " You have told us that before," was the remark. In days of old they used to put an obnoxious brother into a pit, and sell him to the Ishmaelites.—I became very intimate with Townley, who liked me because I was so fond of art. I have stayed with him for days, both in London and in the country; indeed, I was in his house when he died.

Sir Thomas Lawrence told me, that when he, in his boyhood, had received a prize from the Society of Arts, he went with it into the parlour where his brothers and sisters were sitting; but that not one of them would take the slightest notice of it; and that he was so mortified by their affected indifference, that he ran up stairs to his own room, and burst into tears.

On coming home late one night, I found Sir Thomas Lawrence in the street, hovering about my door, and waiting for my return. He immediately began the tale of his distress,— telling me that he was in pressing want of a large sum of money, and that he depended on my assistance, being sure that I would not like to see the President of the Royal Academy a bankrupt. I replied that I would try what I could do for him next morning. Accordingly, I went early to Lord Dudley.* " As you," I said, " can command thousands and thousands

* See p. 108 and *n.—Ed.*

of pounds, and have a truly feeling heart, I want you to help a friend of mine,—not, however, by a gift, but either by a loan, or by purchasing some valuable articles which he has to sell." Dudley, on learning the particulars, accompanied me to Sir Thomas's house, where we looked at several pictures which he wished to dispose of in order to meet the present difficulty. Most of them were early pictures of the Italian school, and, though valuable, not pleasing perhaps to any except artists. Dudley bought one of them (a Raphael, in his first style, as it was called, and probably was), giving, I believe, more than a thousand guineas for it; and he lent Sir Thomas, on a bond, a very considerable sum besides. No doubt, if Lawrence had lived, he would have repaid Lord Dudley by instalments; but he died soon after, and not a penny was ever paid back. This to so very wealthy a man as Dudley was of no consequence; and I dare say he never thought about it at all.—Sir Thomas at the time of his death was a good deal in my debt; nor was I ever repaid.—He used to purchase works of art, especially drawings of the old masters, at immense prices; he was careless in keeping accounts; and he was very generous: hence his difficulties, which were every now and then occurring.

When I mentioned to Mrs. Siddons the anecdote of "Lawrence and his prize," she said, "Alas! after I became celebrated, none of my sisters loved me as they did before."

Mrs. Siddons told me, that one night as she stepped into her carriage to return home from the theatre, Sheridan suddenly jumped in after her. "Mr. Sheridan," she said, "I trust that you will behave with all propriety: if you do not, I shall immediately let down the glass, and desire the servant to show you out." Sheridan *did* behave with all propriety: "but," continued Mrs. Siddons, "as soon as we had reached my house in Marlborough Street, and the footman had opened the carriage-door,—only think! the provoking wretch bolted out in the greatest haste, and slunk away, as if anxious to escape unseen."

After she had left the stage, Mrs. Siddons, from the want of excitement, was never happy. When I was sitting with her of an afternoon, she would say, "Oh, dear! this is the time I used to be thinking of going to the theatre: first came the pleasure of dressing for my part; and then the pleasure of acting it: but that is all over now."

When a grand public dinner was given to John Kemble on his quitting the stage, Mrs. Siddons said to me, "Well, perhaps in the next world women will be more valued than they are in this." She alluded to the comparatively little sensation which had been produced by her own retirement from the boards: and doubtless she was a far, far greater performer than John Kemble.

Combe* recollected having seen Mrs. Siddons, when a very young woman, standing by the side of her father's stage, and knocking a pair of snuffers against a candlestick, to imitate the sound of a windmill, during the representation of some Harlequin-piece.

John Kemble was often very amusing when he had had a good deal of wine. He and two friends were returning to town in an open carriage from the Priory (Lord Abercorn's), where they had dined; and as they were waiting for change at a toll-gate, Kemble, to the amazement of the toll-keeper, called out in the tone of Rolla, " We seek no *change;* and, least of all, such *change* as he would bring us."†

* Combe had conceived a violent dislike to Mrs. Siddons,—why I know not. In a passage of his best work he studiously avoids the mention of her name;—

> " The Drama's children strut and play,
> In borrow'd parts, their lives away;—
> And then they share the oblivious lot;
> Smith will, like Cibber, be forgot!
> Cibber with fascinating art
> Could wake the pulses of the heart;
> But hers is an expiring name,
> And darling Smith's will be the same."
>
> > *The Tour of Doctor Syntax in Search of the Picturesque,* p. 229, third ed. 1813.

The " darling Smith " was the late Mrs. Bartley.—Mrs. Siddons used to say that the public had a sort of pleasure in mortifying their old favourites by setting up new idols; that she herself had been three times threatened with an eclipse,—first by means of Miss Brunton (afterwards Lady Craven), next by means of Miss Smith, and lastly by means of Miss O'Neil: " nevertheless," she added, " I am not yet extinguished." [In Dyce's own copy of the 3rd edition at South Kensington, there is a manuscript note in his own hand after " Miss Brunton (afterwards Lady Craven)," saying that this should read *Mrs. Merry.—Ed.*]

† *Pizarro,* act ii. sc. 2 (where it is " —— as *they* would bring us ").

When Kemble was living at Lausanne, he used to feel rather jealous of Mont Blanc; he disliked to hear people always asking, " How does Mont Blanc look this morning? "

Sir George Beaumont, when a young man, was introduced at Rome to an old painter, who in his youth had known an old painter, who had seen Claude and Gaspar Poussin riding out, in a morning, on mules, and furnished with palettes, &c., to make sketches in the Campagna.

Three Irishmen (I am glad that they were not Englishmen) went up Vesuvius. They stopped at the hermitage to refresh themselves; and while they were drinking lachrima Christi there, the Emperor and Empress of Austria arrived. The three Irishmen positively refused to admit them; but afterwards, on being told that a lady was outside, they offered to give up half the apartment. Upon this, the attendants of the Emperor (though against his wish) speedily cleared the hermitage of the three Irishmen, who, in a great passion, proceeded up to the crater. As they were coming down again, they met the royal personages, whom they abused most heartily, calling the Empress a variety of names under her bonnet. No notice of all this was ever taken by the Emperor: but, the story having got wind immediately, the three Irishmen thought it best to decamp next morning from

Naples, their conduct having excited the highest indignation among the British who were resident there.—I once told this anecdote at Lord Lonsdale's table, when Lord Eldon and Lord Castlereagh were present; and the remark of Lord Castlereagh was, " I am sorry to say that it is too true."

The Colosseum in the Regent's Park is a noble building,—finer than any thing among the remains of ancient architectural art in Italy. It is ridiculous to hear Englishmen who have been at Rome talking with such rapture of the ancient buildings they have seen there: in fact, the old Romans were but indifferent architects.

Georgiana Duchess of Devonshire was not so beautiful as she was fascinating: her beauty was not that of features, but of expression. Every body knows her poem, *The Passage of the Mountain of St. Gothard;* she wrote also what is much less known, a novel called *The Sylph.** Gaming was the rage during her day: she indulged in it, and was made miserable by her debts. A faro-table was kept by Martindale, at which the Duchess and other high fashionables used to play. Sheridan said that the Duchess and Martindale had agreed that whatever they two won from each other should be sometimes *double*, sometimes *treble*, the sum which it was called; and Sheridan

* 1788. 2 vols.

137

assured me that he had handed the Duchess into her carriage when she was literally sobbing at her losses,—she perhaps having lost 1500*l.*, when it was supposed to be only 500*l.*

General Fitzpatrick said that the Duke's love for her grew quite cool a month after their marriage; that she had many sighing swains at her feet,—among others, the Prince of Wales, who chose to believe that she smiled upon Lord Grey; and hence the hatred which the Prince bore to him.

The Duke, when walking home from Brookes's about day-break (for he did not relish the gaieties at Devonshire House) used frequently to pass the stall of a cobbler who had already commenced his work. As they were the only persons stirring in that quarter, they always saluted each other. " Good *night*, friend," said the Duke. " Good *morning*, sir," said the cobbler.

The Duchess was dreadfully hurt at the novel *A Winter in London:** it contained various anecdotes concerning her, which had been picked up from her confidential attendants; and she thought, of course, that the little great world in which she lived was intimately acquainted with all her proceedings. " Never read that book, for it has helped to kill me," were her words to a very near relative.

I introduced Sir Walter Scott to Madame

* In 3 vols., by T. S. Surr. The Duchess figures in it under the name of the Duchess of Belgrave.

D'Arblay, having taken him with me to her house. She had not heard that he was lame; and when he limped towards a chair, she said, " Dear me, Sir Walter, I hope you have not met with an accident? " He answered, " An accident, madam, nearly as old as my birth."

At the time when Scott and Byron were the two *lions* of London, Hookham Frere observed, " Great poets formerly (Homer and Milton) were blind; now they are lame."

One forenoon Scott was sitting for his bust to Chantrey, who was quite in despair at the dull and heavy expression of his countenance. Suddenly, Fuller ("Jack Fuller," the then buffoon of the House of Commons) was announced by a servant; and, as suddenly, Scott's face was lighted up to that pitch of animation which the sculptor desired, and which he made all haste to avail himself of.

After dining at my house, Sir Walter (then Mr.) Scott accompanied me to a party given by Lady Jersey. We met Sheridan there, who put the question to Scott in express terms, " Pray, Mr. Scott, did you, or did you not, write *Waverley?* " Scott replied, " *On my honour,* I did not." Now, though Scott may perhaps be justified for returning an answer in the negative, I cannot think that he is to be excused for strengthening it with " on my honour."

There is a very pleasing spirit of kindness in Scott's *Life of Swift* and *Lives of the Novelists;* he endeavours to place every body's actions in the most favourable light.

As a *story*, his *Lady of the Lake* is delightful.*
—On the whole, his *poetry* is too carelessly written
to suit my taste; but parts of it are very happy.

Why there should be evil in the world is
indeed a mystery. Milton attempts to answer
the question; but he has not done it satisfactorily.
The three acutest men with whom I was ever
acquainted, Sir James Mackintosh, Malthus,
and Bobus Smith, were all agreed that the
attributes of the Deity must be in some respects
limited, else there would be no sin and misery.

When I lived in the Temple, Mackintosh and
Richard Sharp used to come to my chambers, and
stay there for hours, talking metaphysics. One
day they were so intent on their " first cause,"
" spirit," and " matter," that they were
unconscious of my having left them, paid a
visit, and returned! I was a little angry at this,
and, to show my indifference about them, I
sat down and wrote letters, without taking any
notice of them.

Mackintosh told me that he had received in
his youth comparatively little instruction,—
whatever learning he possessed he owed to himself. He had a prodigious memory, and could
repeat by heart more of Cicero than you would
easily believe. His knowledge of Greek was

* I have heard Wordsworth say that it was one of the most charming
stories ever invented by a poet.

slender. I never met a man with a fuller mind than Mackintosh,—such readiness on all subjects, such a talker!*

I once travelled with him on the Continent; yet, in spite of his delightful conversation, some how or other we did not hit it off well. At Lausanne my sister and I went to see Gibbon's house; and, borrowing the last volume of the *Decline and Fall*, we read the concluding passages of it on the very spot where they were written. But such an amusement was not to Mackintosh's taste: he meanwhile was trotting about, and making inquiries concerning the salaries of professors, &c. &c. When we were leaving Geneva, I could not find my *sac-de-nuit*, and was forced to buy a new one. On stepping into the carriage, I saw there, to my surprise, the lost article, which Mackintosh had very coolly taken and had stuffed with recently-purchased books.

Lord Ellenborough had infinite wit. When the income-tax was imposed, he said that Lord Kenyon (who was not very nice in his habits) intended, in consequence of it, to lay down— his pocket-handkerchief.

A lawyer one day pleading before him, and using several times the expression "my unfortunate client," Lord Ellenborough suddenly interrupted him,—" There, sir, the court is with you."

* But cf. Hazlitt on Mackintosh, in *The Spirit of the Age*, 1825.— *Ed*.

Lord Ellenborough was once about to go on the circuit, when Lady E. said that she should like to accompany him. He replied that he had no objections, provided she did not encumber the carriage with bandboxes, which were his utter abhorrence,—" No trumpery, madam, no trumpery." They set off. During the first day's journey, Lord Ellenborough, happening to stretch his legs, struck his feet against something below the seat. He discovered that it was a bandbox. His indignation is not to be described. Up went the window, and out went the bandbox. The coachman stopped; and the footmen, thinking that the bandbox had tumbled out of the window by some extraordinary chance, were going to pick it up, when Lord Ellenborough furiously called out, " Drive on!" The bandbox accordingly was left by a ditch-side. Having reached the county-town where he was to officiate as judge, Lord Ellenborough proceeded to array himself for his appearance in the court-house. " Now," said he, " where's my wig,—where *is* my wig ? " " My lord," replied his attendant, " it was thrown out of the carriage-window."

The English highwaymen of former days (indeed, the race is now extinct) were remarkably well-bred personages. Thomas Grenville, while travelling with Lord Derby; and Lord Tankerville, while travelling with his father; were attacked by highwaymen: on both occasions, six or seven shots were exchanged between them and the highwaymen; and when the parties assailed had expended all their ammunition, the highwaymen came up to them, and took their purses in the politest manner possible.

Foreigners have more romance in their natures than we English. Fuseli, during his later years, used to be a very frequent visitor of Lady Guilford, at Putney Hill. In the grounds belonging to her villa there was a statue of Flora holding a wreath of flowers. Fuseli would frequently place in the wreath a slip of paper, containing some pretty sentiment, or some expressions of kindness, intended for Lady Guilford's daughters; who would take it away, and replace it by another of the same kind. When one of these ladies told me this, the tears were in her eyes.

The three great curses of Ireland are, Absenteeism, Middlemen, and the Protestant Establishment.

A man who attempts to read all the new publications must often do as a flea does—*skip*.

Such is the eagerness of the human mind for excitement,—for *an event*,—that people generally have a sort of satisfaction in reading the deaths of their friends in the newspapers. I don't mean that a man would not be shocked to read there the death of his child, or of his dearest friend; but that he feels a kind of pleasure in reading that of an acquaintance, because it gives him something to talk about with every body on whom he may have to call during the day.

You remember the passage in *King Lear*,—a passage which Mrs. Siddons said that she never could read without shedding tears,—

" Do not laugh at me;
For, as I am a man, I think this lady
To be my child Cordelia."

Something of the same kind happened in my own family. A gentleman, a near relation of mine, was on his death-bed, and his intellect much impaired, when his daughter, whom he had not seen for a considerable time, entered the room. He looked at her with the greatest earnestness, and then exclaimed, " I think I should know *this lady* ": but *his* recognition went no further.

One morning I had a visit from Lancaster,* whom I had never before seen. The moment he entered the room, he began to inform me of his distresses, and burst into tears. He was

* Joseph Lancaster, the educationist.—*Ed.*

unable, he said, to carry on his school for want of money,—he owed some hundred pounds to his landlord,—he had been to the Chancellor of the Exchequer, who would do nothing for him, &c. &c.; and he requested me to go and see his school. I went; and was so delighted with what I saw (the system of monitors, &c.), that I immediately lent him the sum which he stood in need of; and he put his title-deeds into my hands. I never was repaid one farthing of that money; indeed, on finding that Lancaster owed much larger sums both to William Allen and to Joseph Fox, I forbore urging my claims, and returned the title-deeds.*

George Selwyn, as every body knows, delighted in seeing executions; he never missed *being in at a death* at Tyburn. When Lord Holland (the father of Charles Fox) was confined to bed by a dangerous illness, he was informed by his servant that Mr. Selwyn had recently called to inquire for him. " On his next visit," said Lord Holland, " be sure you let him in, whether I am alive or a corpse; for, if I am alive, *I* shall

* " I was well acquainted with Lancaster. He once came to me in great agitation, and complained bitterly that ' they wanted to put him under the control of a committee, who were to allow him 365*l.* a-year,' &c. &c. I knew how thoughtless and improvident he had been, driving about the country with four horses, and doing many other foolish things; and I could not take that view of his case which he wished me to take. This offended him: he burst into tears, and left the room, declaring that he would never again come near me. He went to America, and died there in obscurity,—a man who, if he had only possessed prudence, might have had statues erected to him."—*Maltby*.

have great pleasure in seeing *him;* and if I am a corpse, *he will have great pleasure in seeing me*." —The late Lord Holland told me this.

Payne Knight was seized with an utter loathing of life, and destroyed himself. He had complaints which were very painful, and his nerves were completely shattered. Shortly before his death, he would come to me of an evening, and tell me how sick he was of existence. He had recourse to the strongest prussic acid; and, I understand, *he was dead before it touched his lips*.*

Two of the most enchanting lyrics in our language are Collins's *Ode to Evening*, and Coleridge's *Love*. The former could not possibly be improved by the addition of rhyme. The latter is so exquisitely musical, that I had often repeated it to myself before I discovered that the first and third lines of each stanza do not rhyme.

Coleridge was a marvellous talker. One morning, when Hookham Frere also breakfasted with me, Coleridge talked for three hours without intermission about poetry, and so admirably, that I wish every word he uttered had been written down.

But sometimes his harangues were quite unintelligible, not only to myself, but to others.

* In his third edition, Dyce, though maintaining the accuracy of his reporting of Rogers, adds a note to the effect that Knight, according to his relatives, died of apoplexy.—*Ed.*

Wordsworth and I called upon him one fore-noon, when he was in a lodging off Pall Mall. He talked uninterruptedly for about two hours, during which Wordsworth listened to him with profound attention, every now and then nodding his head as if in assent. On quitting the lodging, I said to Wordsworth, " Well, for my own part, I could not make head or tail of Coleridge's oration: pray, did you understand it? " " Not one syllable of it," was Wordsworth's reply.*

Speaking of composition, Coleridge said most beautifully, " What comes from the heart goes to the heart."

Coleridge spoke and wrote† very disparagingly of Mackintosh: but Mackintosh, who had not a particle of envy or jealousy in his nature, did full justice, on all occasions, to the great powers of Coleridge.

Southey used to say that " the moment any thing assumed the shape of a duty, Coleridge felt himself incapable of discharging it."

In all his domestic relations Southey was the most amiable of men; but he had no general philanthropy; he was what you call *a cold man*. He was never happy except when reading a book

* Wordsworth once observed to me: " What is somewhere stated in print,—that I said, ' Coleridge was the only person whose intellect ever astonished me,' is quite true. His conversation was even finer in his youth than in his later days; for, as he advanced in life, he became a little dreamy and hyper-metaphysical."

† See, in Coleridge's *Poet. Works, The Two Round Spaces on the Tombstone*.

or making one. Coleridge once said to me, " I can't *think* of Southey, without seeing him either mending or using a pen." I spent some time with him at Lord Lonsdale's, in company with Wordsworth and others; and while the rest of the party were walking about, talking, and amusing themselves, Southey preferred sitting solus in the library. " How *cold* he is! " was the exclamation of Wordsworth,—himself so joyous and communicative.

Southey told me that he had read Spenser through about *thirty* times, and that he could not read Pope through *once*. He thought meanly of Virgil; so did Coleridge; and so, at one time, did Wordsworth. When I lately mentioned to Wordsworth an unfavourable opinion which he had formerly expressed to me about a passage of Virgil, " Oh," he said, " we used to talk a great deal of nonsense in those days."

Early in the present century, I set out on a tour in Scotland, accompanied by my sister; but an accident which happened to her prevented us from going as far as we had intended. During our excursion we fell in with Wordsworth, Miss Wordsworth, and Coleridge, who were, at the same time, making a tour in a vehicle that looked very like a cart.* Wordsworth and Coleridge were entirely occupied in talking about poetry; and the whole care of looking out for cottages where they might get refreshment and

* 1803. See Dorothy Wordsworth's *Journals.—Ed.*

pass the night, as well as of seeing their poor horse fed and littered, devolved upon Miss Wordsworth. She was a most delightful person, —so full of talent, so simple-minded, and so modest! If I am not mistaken, Coleridge proved so impracticable a travelling-companion, that Wordsworth and his sister were at last obliged to separate from him.* During that tour they met with Scott, who repeated to them a portion of his then unpublished *Lay;* which Wordsworth, as might be expected, did not greatly admire.†

I do indeed regret that Wordsworth has printed only fragments of his sister's *Journal:*‡ it is most excellent, and ought to have been published entire.

I was walking with Lord Lonsdale on the terrace at Lowther Castle, when he said, " I wish I could do something for poor Campbell." My rejoinder was, " I wish you would do something for poor Wordsworth, who is in such

* " Coleridge," writes Wordsworth, " was at that time in bad spirits, and somewhat too much in love with his own dejection; and he departed from us, as is recorded in my sister's journal, soon after we left Loch Lomond." *Memoirs of Wordsworth*, i. 207.

† In my memoranda of Wordsworth's conversation I find this: " From Sir Walter Scott's earliest poems, *The Eve of St. John*, &c. I did not suppose that he possessed the power which he afterwards displayed, especially in his novels. Coleridge's *Christabel* no doubt gave him the idea of writing long ballad-poems: Dr. Stoddart had a very wicked memory, and repeated various passages of it (then unpublished) to Scott. Part of the *Lay of the Last Minstrel* was recited to me by Scott while it was yet in manuscript; and I did not expect that it would make much sensation: but I was mistaken; for it went up like a balloon."

‡ A large portion of it has since been printed in the *Memoirs* of her brother.

straitened circumstances, that he and his family deny themselves animal food several times a week." Lord Lonsdale was the more inclined to assist Wordsworth, because the Wordsworth family had been hardly used by the preceding Lord Lonsdale; and he eventually proved one of his kindest friends.

What a noble-minded person Lord Lonsdale was! I have received from him, in this room, hundreds of pounds for the relief of literary men.

I never attempted to write a sonnet, because I do not see why a man, if he has any thing worth saying, should be tied down to fourteen lines. Wordsworth perhaps appears to most advantage in a sonnet, because its strict limits prevent him from running into that wordiness to which he is somewhat prone. Don't imagine from what I have just said, that I mean to disparage Wordsworth: he deserves all his fame.

There are passages in Wordsworth where I can trace his obligations to Usher's *Clio*.*

Hoppner was a painter of decided genius. Some of his portraits are equal to any modern portraits; and his Venus is certainly fine.

He had an awful temper,—the most spiteful person I ever knew! He and I were members of a club called the *Council of Trent* (so named from its consisting of thirty); and because, on one occasion, I was interesting myself about the

---

* *Clio, or a Discourse on Taste.*

admission of an artist whom Hoppner disliked, Hoppner wrote me a letter full of the bitterest reproach. Yet he had his good qualities. He had been a singing-boy at Windsor,* and consequently was allowed " the run of the royal kitchen "; but some time after his marriage (and, it was supposed, through the ill offices of West) that favour was withdrawn; and in order to conceal the matter from his wife, who, he knew, would be greatly vexed at it, Hoppner occasionally, after secretly pocketing a roll to dine upon, would go out for the day, and on his return pretend that he had been dining at Windsor.

He and Gifford were the dearest friends in the world; and yet they were continually falling out and abusing each other. One morning, Hoppner, having had some little domestic quarrel with Mrs. Hoppner, exclaimed very vehemently, " Is not a man to be pitied who has such a wife and such a friend " (meaning Gifford)?

His wife and daughter were always grumbling, because, when *he* was asked to the Duchess of ——'s or to Lord ——'s, *they* were not invited also; and he once said to them, " I might as well attempt to take the York waggon with me as you." Indeed, society is so constituted in England, that it is useless for celebrated artists to think of bringing their families into the highest circles, where themselves are admitted

* In consequence of the sweetness of his voice, he was made a chorister in the Royal Chapel. His mother was one of the German attendants at the Palace. See A. Cunningham's *Lives of British Painters*, v. 242.

only on account of their genius. Their wives and daughters must be content to remain at home.

Gifford was extremely indignant at an article on his translation of Juvenal which appeared in *The Critical Review;* and he put forth a very angry answer to it,—a large quarto pamphlet. I lent my copy to Byron, and he never returned it. One passage in that pamphlet is curious, because it describes, what Gifford was himself eventually to become,—a reviewer; who is compared to a huge toad sitting under a stone: and besides, the passage is very picturesque. [" During my apprenticeship, I enjoyed perhaps as many places as Scrub, though I suspect they were not altogether so dignified: the chief of them was that of a planter of cabbages in a bit of ground which my master held near the town. It was the decided opinion of Panurge that the life of a cabbage-planter was the safest and pleasantest in the world. I found it safe enough, I confess, but not altogether pleasant; and therefore took every opportunity of attending to what I liked better, which happened to be, watching the actions of insects and reptiles, and, among the rest, of a huge toad. I never loved toads, but I never molested them; for my mother had early bid me remember, that every living thing had the same Maker as myself; and the words always rang in my ears. This toad, then, who had taken up his residence under a hollow stone in a hedge of blind nettles, I used to watch for hours together. It was a lazy, lumpish animal, that squatted on its belly, and perked up its hideous head with two glazed eyes, precisely like a Critical Reviewer. In this posture, perfectly satisfied with itself, it would remain as if it were a part of the stone which sheltered it, till the cheerful buzzing of some winged insect provoked it to give signs of life. The dead glare of its eyes then brightened into a vivid lustre, and it awkwardly shuffled to the entrance of its cell, and opened its detestable mouth to snap the passing fly or honey-bee. Since I have marked the manners of the Critical Reviewers, these passages of my youth have often occurred to me." *An Examination of the Strictures of the Critical Reviewers on the Translation of Juvenal by W. Gifford, Esq.*, p. 101, third ed. 1804.]

When the *Quarterly Review* was first projected, Gifford sent Hoppner to my house with a message requesting me to become a contributor to it; which I declined.

That odd being, Dr. Monsey (Physician to the Royal Hospital, Chelsea),* used to hide his banknotes in various holes and corners of his house. One evening, before going out, he

---

* In which capacity he is said to have invented an original method of extracting teeth. One end of a strong piece of catgut was attached to the tooth, the other to a perforated bullet, which was then fired from a pistol. Dr. Monsey is reputed to have thus dealt successfully with his own teeth; but it is not recorded that any of his patients had the enterprise to follow his example.—*Ed.*

carefully deposited a bundle of them among the coals in the parlour-grate, where the fire was ready for lighting. Presently, his housekeeper came into the parlour, with some of her female friends, to have a comfortable cup of tea; and she was in the act of lighting the fire when the doctor luckily returned, and rescued his notes. A friend of mine, who had been intimate with Monsey, assured me that this was fact.

Bishop Horsley one day met Monsey in the Park. "These are dreadful times!" said Horsley: "not only do deists abound, but,—would you think it, doctor?—some people deny that there is a God!"—"I can tell you," replied Monsey, "what is equally strange,—some people believe that there are three." Horsley immediately walked away.

An Englishman and a Frenchman having quarrelled, they were to fight a duel; and, that they might have a better chance of missing one another, they agreed that it should take place in a room perfectly dark. The Englishman groped his way to the hearth, fired up the chimney, and brought down—the Frenchman. (Whenever I tell this story in Paris, I make *the Frenchman* fire up the chimney.)

A certain man of pleasure about London received a challenge from a young gentleman of his acquaintance; and they met at the appointed place. Just before the signal for firing was given, the man of pleasure rushed up to his

antagonist, embraced him, and vehemently pro-
tested that " he could not lift his arm *against his
own flesh and blood!* " The young gentleman,
though he had never heard any imputation
cast upon his mother's character, was so much
staggered, that (as the ingenious man of pleasure
had foreseen) no duel took place.

Humphrey Howarth, the surgeon, was called
out, and made his appearance in the field stark
naked, to the astonishment of the challenger,
who asked him what he meant. " I know,"
said H., " that if any part of the clothing is
carried into the body by a gunshot wound,
festering ensues; and therefore I have met
you thus." His antagonist declared, that fighting with a man *in puris naturalibus* would be
quite ridiculous; and accordingly they parted
without further discussion.

Lord Alvanley on returning home, after his
duel with young O'Connel, gave a guinea to
the hackney-coachman who had driven him
out and brought him back. The man, surprised
at the largeness of the sum, said, " My lord, I
only took you to ――." Alvanley interrupted
him, " My friend, the guinea is *for bringing me
back*, not for taking me out."

I was on a visit to Lord Bath at Longleat,
when I received a letter from Beckford* inviting

* In the following terms : " If Mr. Rogers continues to feel any in-
clination to hear the secrets of the prison house of Eblis unfolded, he
may perhaps be inspired to appoint a day and a night for the purpose.
Nothing would afford the Abbot of Fonthill higher gratification."—
Clayden : Rogers & his Contemporaries, V. I., pp. 251-2.—*Ed.*

me to Fonthill. I went there, and stayed three days. On arriving at the gate, I was informed that neither my servant nor my horses could be admitted, but that Mr. Beckford's attendants and horses should be at my service. The other visitors at that time were Smith, who published *Views in Italy*,* and a French ecclesiastic, a very elegant and accomplished man. During the day we used to drive about the beautiful grounds in pony-chaises. In the evening Beckford would amuse us by reading one of his unpublished works; or he would extemporise on the pianoforte, producing the most novel and charming melodies (which, by the by, his daughter, the Duchess of Hamilton, can do also).

I was struck rather by the refinement than by the magnificence of the hospitality at Fonthill. I slept in a bedroom which opened into a gallery where lights were kept burning the whole night. In that gallery was a picture of St. Antonio, to which it was said that Beckford would sometimes steal and pay his devotions.

Beckford read to me the two unprinted episodes to *Vathek;* and they are extremely fine, but very objectionable on account of their subjects. Indeed, they show that the mind of the author was to a certain degree diseased. The one is the story of a prince and princess, a brother and sister,   *   *   *   *
The other is the tale of a prince who is violently enamoured of a lady; and who, after pursuing

* *Select Views in Italy, with Descriptions, Fr. and English,* by John Smith, 1792–6, 2 vols. 4to.

her through various countries, at last overtakes her only to find her a corpse.　*　*　*
In one of these tales there is an exquisite description of a voyage down the Nile.

Beckford is the author of two burlesque novels, —*Azemia** and *The Elegant Enthusiast*. I have a copy of the former, which he presented to me.

He read to me another tale which he had written—a satirical one. It was in French, and about a man who was ridiculously fond of dogs, &c. &c. I have been told that a part of his own life was shadowed out in it. This tale he never printed. In fact, he had no wish to obtain literary reputation: he despised it.

I have seen Beckford shed tears while talking

---

* *Azemia: a descriptive and sentimental Novel, interspersed with pieces of Poetry. By Jacquetta Agneta Mariana Jenks, of Bellegrove Priory in Wales. Dedicated to the Right Honourable Lady Harriet Marlow. To which are added, Criticisms anticipated*, 1797, 2 vols.— *Modern Novel Writing, or the Elegant Enthusiast; and Interesting Emotions of Arabella Bloomville. A Rhapsodical Romance; interspersed with Poetry. By the Right Hon. Lady Harriet Marlow*, 1796, 2 vols.—" Talked of Beckford's two *mock* novels, ' Agemia ' [*Azemia*] and the ' Elegant Enthusiast,' which he wrote to ridicule the novels written by his sister, Mrs. Harvey (I think), who read these parodies on herself quite innocently, and only now and then suspecting that they were meant to laugh at her, saying, Why, I vow and protest, here is my grotto, &c. &c. In the ' Elegant Enthusiast ' the heroine writes a song which she sings at a masquerade, and which produces such an effect, that my Lord Mahogany, in the character of a Milestone, bursts into tears. *It is in ' Agemia ' [Azemia] that all the heroes and heroines are killed at the conclusion by a supper of stewed lampreys.*" Moore's *Memoirs*, &c. ii. 197. As to the catastrophe of *Azemia*, Moore was misinformed; that tale has nothing about a fatal supper of stewed lampreys: there is, however, in the second volume of *The Elegant Enthusiast* a similar incident, " owing to a copper stew-pan in which some celery had been cooked." Both these novels are much in the style of Beckford's *Memoirs of Extraordinary Painters*, but greatly inferior to that strange production, which itself is unworthy of the author of *Vathek*.

of his deceased wife. His eldest daughter (Mrs. Orde), who has been long dead, was both in appearance and disposition a perfect angel. Her delight was, not to be admired herself, but to witness the admiration which her sister (the Duchess of Hamilton) never failed to excite.

Beckford was eventually reduced to such straits, that he was obliged to part with his pictures, one by one. The last picture which he sold to the National Gallery was Bellini's portrait of the Doge of Venice. It was hung up the very day on which Beckford died: the Duke of Hamilton wrote a letter to me, requesting that it might be returned to the family; but his application came too late.

When Porson dined with me, I used to keep him within bounds; but I frequently met him at various houses where he got completely drunk. He would not scruple to return to the dining-room, after the company had left it, pour into a tumbler the drops remaining in the wine-glasses, and drink off the omnium gatherum.

I once took him to an evening-party at William Spencer's, where he was introduced to several women of fashion, Lady Crewe, &c., who were very anxious to see the great Grecian. How do you suppose he entertained them? Chiefly by reciting an immense quantity of old forgotten Vauxhall songs. He was far from sober, and at last talked so oddly, that they all retired from him, except Lady Crewe, who boldly kept her ground. I recollect her saying to him, " Mr. Porson, *that* joke you have borrowed from Joe Miller," and his rather angry reply, " Madam, it is *not* in Joe Miller; you will not find it either in the preface or in the body of that work, no, nor in the index." I brought him home as far as Piccadilly, where, I am sorry to add, I left him sick in the middle of the street.

When any one told Porson that he intended to *publish* a book, Porson would say, " Remember that two parties must agree on that point,—you and the reader."

I asked him what time it would take him to translate *The Iliad* literally and correctly into English prose. He answered, " At least ten years."

He used to say that something may be pleaded as a sort of excuse for the wickedness of the worst characters in Shakespeare. For instance, Iago is tortured by suspicions that Othello has been too intimate with his wife; Richard the Third, the murderer of children, has been bitterly taunted by one of the young princes, &c.

" If I had a carriage," said Porson, " and if I saw a well-dressed person on the road, I would always invite him in, and learn of him what I could." Such was his love of knowledge!

He was fond of repeating these lines,* and wrote them out for me;

* From Garnett's *Tour in Scotland*, vol. ii. 227. They were found in an album kept at the inn at Lanark.

" What fools are mankind,
    And how strangely inclin'd,
    To come from all places
    With horses and chaises,
    By day and by dark,
    To the falls of Lanark!
    For, good people, after all,
    What is a water-fall?
    It comes roaring and grumbling,
    And leaping and tumbling,
    And hopping and skipping,
    And foaming and dripping;
    And struggling and toiling,
    And bubbling and boiling;
    And beating and jumping,
    And bellowing and thumping.
    I have much more to say upon
    Both Linn and Bonniton;
    But the trunks are tied on,
    And I must be gone."

These lines evidently suggested to Southey his playful verses on *The Cataract of Lodore*.

The following anecdotes of Porson were communicated to me, in conversation, at various times, by the late Mr. William Maltby,—the schoolfellow, and, throughout life, the most confidential friend of Mr. Rogers:—

I first saw Porson at the sale of Toup's library in 1784, and was introduced to him soon after.

I was on the most intimate terms with him for the last twenty years of his life. In spite of all his faults and failings, it was impossible not to admire his integrity and his love of truth.

Porson declared that he learned nothing while a schoolboy at Eton. " Before I went there," he said, " I could nearly repeat by heart all the books which we used to read in the school." The only thing in his Eton course which he recollected with pleasure was—rat-hunting! he used to talk with delight of the rat-hunts in the Long Hall.

During the earlier part of his career, he accepted the situation of tutor to a young gentleman in the Isle of Wight; but he was soon forced to relinquish that office, in consequence of having been found drunk in a ditch or a turnip-field.

Porter was his favourite beverage at breakfast. One Sunday morning meeting Dr. Goodall (Provost of Eton), he said, " Where are you going?" " To church."—" Where is Mrs. Goodall?" " At breakfast."—" Very well; I'll go and breakfast with her." Porson accordingly presented himself before Mrs. Goodall; and being asked what he chose to take, he said " porter." It was sent for, pot after pot; and the sixth pot was just being carried into the house when Dr. Goodall returned from church.

At one period of his life he was in such straitened circumstances, that he would go without dinner for a couple of days. However, when a dinner came in his way, he would eat very heartily (mutton was his favourite dish), and lay in, as he used to say, a stock of provision. He has subsisted for three weeks upon a guinea.

Sometimes, at a later period, when he was able enough to pay for a dinner, he chose, in a fit of abstinence, to go without one. I have asked him to stay and dine with me; and he has replied, "Thank you, no; I dined yesterday."

At dinner, and after it, he preferred port to any other wine.* He disliked both tea and coffee.

Porson would sit up drinking all night, without seeming to feel any bad effects from it. Horne Tooke told me that he once asked Porson to dine with him in Richmond Buildings; and, as he knew that Porson had not been in bed for the three preceding nights, he expected to get rid of him at a tolerably early hour. Porson, however, kept Tooke up the whole night; and in the morning, the latter, in perfect despair, said, " Mr. Porson, I am engaged to meet a friend at breakfast at a coffee-house in Leicester Square."—" Oh," replied Porson, " I will go with you "; and he accordingly did so. Soon after they had reached the coffee-house, Tooke contrived to slip out, and running home, ordered his servant not to let Mr. Porson in, even if he should attempt to batter down the door. " A man," observed Tooke, " who could sit up

* But he was not particular. *Cf.* his favourite song, upon carouses :
When wine is gone, and money spent,
Then small-beer is most excellent.—*Ed*.

four nights successively might have sat up forty."*

Tooke used to say that " Porson would drink ink rather than not drink at all." Indeed, he would drink any thing. He was sitting with a gentleman, after dinner, in the chambers of a mutual friend, a Templar, who was then ill and confined to bed. A servant came into the room, sent thither by his master for a bottle of embrocation which was on the chimney-piece. " I drank it an hour ago," said Porson.

When Hoppner the painter was residing in a cottage a few miles from London, Porson, one afternoon, unexpectedly arrived there. Hoppner said that he could not offer him dinner, as Mrs. H. had gone to town, and had carried with her the key of the closet which contained the wine. Porson, however, declared that he would be content with a mutton-chop, and beer from the next alehouse; and accordingly stayed to dine. During the evening Porson said, " I am quite certain that Mrs. Hoppner keeps some nice bottle, for her private drinking, in her own bedroom; so, pray, try if you can lay your hands on it." His host assured him that Mrs. H. had no such secret stores; but Porson insisting that a search should be made, a bottle was at

* In Stephens's *Memoirs of Horne Tooke*, vol. ii. 315, is an account of Porson's rudeness to Tooke while dining with him one day at Wimbledon, and of Tooke's silencing and triumphing over him by making him dead drunk with brandy; on which occasion " some expressions of a disagreeable nature are said to have occurred at table."—At that dinner Tooke (as he told Mr. Maltby) asked Porson for a toast; and Porson replied, " I will give you—the man who is in all respects the very reverse of John Horne Tooke."

last discovered in the lady's apartment, to the surprise of Hoppner, and the joy of Porson, who soon finished its contents, pronouncing it to be the best gin he had tasted for a long time. Next day, Hoppner, somewhat out of temper, informed his wife that Porson had drunk every drop of her concealed dram. " Drunk every drop of it! " cried she: " my God, it was spirits-of-wine for the lamp! "

A brother of Bishop Maltby invited Porson and myself to spend the evening at his house, and secretly requested me to take Porson away, if possible, before the morning hours. Accordingly, at twelve o'clock I held up my watch to Porson, saying, " I think it is now full time for us to go home "; and the host, of course, not pressing us to remain longer, away we went. When we got into the street Porson's indignation burst forth: " I hate," he said, " to be turned out of doors like a dog."

At the house of the same gentleman I introduced Cogan to Porson, saying, " This is Mr. Cogan, who is passionately fond of what you have devoted yourself to,—Greek." Porson replied, " If Mr. Cogan is passionately fond of Greek, he must be content to dine on bread and cheese for the remainder of his life."

Gurney (the Baron) had chambers in Essex Court, Temple, under Porson's. One night (or rather, morning) Gurney was awakened by a tremendous thump in the chambers above. Porson had just come home dead drunk, and had fallen on the floor. Having extinguished his candle in the fall, he presently staggered down stairs to relight it; and Gurney heard him keep dodging and poking with the candle at the staircase-lamp for about five minutes, and all the while very lustily cursing the nature of things.

Porson was fond of smoking, and said that when smoking began to go out of fashion, learning began to go out of fashion also.

He was generally ill dressed and dirty. But I never saw him such a figure as he was one day at Leigh and Sotheby's auction-room: he evidently had been rolling in the kennel; and, on inquiry, I found that he was just come from a party (at Robert Heathcote's, I believe), with whom he had been sitting up drinking for two nights.

One forenoon I met Porson in Covent Garden, dressed in a pea-green coat: he had been married* that morning, as I afterwards learned from Raine, for he himself said nothing about it. He was carrying a copy of *Le Moyen de Parvenir*,† which he had just purchased off a stall; and holding it up, he called out jokingly, " These are the sort of books to buy! "

" I was occupied two years," said Porson, " in composing the *Letters to Travis*‡: I received

* " In 1795, R. P. married Mrs. Lunan, who sunk under a decline in 1797." Kidd's *Life of Porson*, p. xv. She was sister to Perry, editor of *The Morning Chronicle*. *The Farington Diary* dates this marriage 1796, and adds that the bride was divorced from her first husband by the law of Scotland, and had several children to maintain.—*Ed*.

† By Béroalde de Verville, one time canon of Tours.—*Ed*.

‡ Letters to Archdeacon Travis on a disputed passage. I John v. 7.—*Ed*.

thirty pounds for them from Egerton; and I am glad to find that he lost sixteen by the publication."

Soon after the *Letters to Travis* were published, Gibbon wrote a note to Porson, requesting the pleasure of his acquaintance. Porson accordingly called upon the great historian, who received him with all kindness and respect. In the course of conversation Gibbon said, " Mr. Porson, I feel truly indebted to you for the *Letters to Travis*, though I must think that occasionally, while praising me, you have mingled a little acid with the sweet. If ever you should take the trouble to read my History over again, I should be much obliged and honoured by any remarks on it which might suggest themselves to you." Porson was highly flattered by Gibbon's having requested this interview, and loved to talk of it. He thought the *Decline and Fall* beyond all comparison the greatest literary production of the eighteenth century, and was in the habit of repeating long passages from it. Yet I have heard him say that " there could not be a better exercise for a schoolboy than to turn a page of it into *English*."

When the *Letters to Travis* first appeared, Rennell said to me, " It is just such a book as the devil would write, if he could hold a pen."

As soon as Gibbon's Autobiography and Miscellaneous Works came out, they were eagerly devoured both by Porson and myself. Neither of us could afford to purchase the quarto edition; so we bought the Dublin reprint in octavo.

There was no cordiality between Porson and Jacob Bryant, for they thought very differently not only on the subject of Troy, but on most other subjects. Bryant used to abuse Porson behind his back; and one day, when he was violently attacking his character, the Bishop of Salisbury, Dr. Douglas, said to him, " Mr. Bryant, you are speaking of a great man; and you should remember, sir, that even the greatest men are not without their failings."

Porson was sometimes very rude in society. My relation, Dr. Maltby (Bishop of Durham), once invited him to meet Paley at dinner. Paley arrived first. When Porson (who had never before seen him) came into the room, he seated himself in an arm-chair, and looking very hard at Paley, said, " I am entitled to this chair, being president of a society for the discovery of truth, of which I happen at present to be the only member." These words were levelled at certain *political* opinions broached in Paley's works.

I have often wondered that Porson did not get into scrapes in those days, when it was so dangerous to express violent political feelings: he would think nothing of toasting " Jack Cade " at a tavern, when he was half-seas-over.

One day after dinner, at Clayton Jennings's house, Captain Ash, who was always ready to warble, burst out, as usual, with a song. Now, Porson hated singing after dinner; and, while Ash was in the middle of his song, an ass happening to bray in the street, Porson interrupted the Captain with " Sir, you have a rival."

He used frequently to regret that he had not gone to America in his youth and settled there. I said, " What would you have done without books? " He answered, " I should have done without them."

At one time he had some thoughts of taking orders, and studied divinity for a year or two. " But," said he, " I found that I should require *about fifty years' reading* to make myself thoroughly acquainted with it,—to satisfy my mind on all points; and therefore I gave it up. There are fellows who go into a pulpit, assuming every thing, and knowing nothing: but *I* would not do so."

He said that every man ought to marry *once*. I observed that every man could not afford to maintain a family. " Oh," replied he, " pap is cheap."

He insisted that all men are born with abilities nearly equal. " Any one," he would say, " might become quite as good a critic as I am, if he would only take the trouble to make himself so. I have made myself what I am by intense labour: sometimes, in order to impress a thing upon my memory, I have read it a dozen times, and transcribed it six."*

He once had occasion to travel to Norwich.

* But *he* was certainly gifted by nature with most extraordinary powers of memory. Dr. Dauney, of Aberdeen, told me that, during a visit to London, he *heard Porson declare* that he could repeat Smollett's *Roderick Random* from beginning to end:—and Mr. Richard Heber assured me that soon after the appearance of the *Essay on Irish Bulls* (the joint production of Edgeworth and his daughter), Porson used, when somewhat tipsy, to recite *whole pages of it verbatim* with great delight.

When the coach arrived there, he was beset by several porters, one offering to carry his portmanteau to his lodging for eighteen-pence, another for a shilling, another for ninepence: upon which, Porson shouldered the portmanteau, and marching off with it, said very gravely to the porters, " Gentlemen, I leave you to settle this dispute among yourselves."—When, however, he went to stay with a friend for only a couple of days or so, he did not encumber himself with a portmanteau: he would merely take a shirt in his pocket, saying, " *Omnia mea mecum porto.*"

The time he wasted in writing notes on the margins of books,—I mean, in writing them with such beauty of penmanship that they rivalled print,—was truly lamentable.* And yet he used those very books most cruelly, whether they were his own, or belonging to others: he would let them lie about his room, covered with dust and all sorts of dirt.—He said that " he possessed more *bad* copies of *good* books than any private gentleman in England."

---

* Such was his rage for calligraphy, that he once offered *to letter the backs* of some of Mr. Richard Heber's vellum-bound classics. " No," said Heber, " I won't let you do that: but I shall be most thankful if you will write into an Athenæus some of those excellent emendations which I have heard from you in conversation." Heber accordingly sent to him Brunck's† interleaved copy of that author (Casaubon's edition); which Porson enriched with many notes.

† This would be the Brunck referred to in Porson's most celebrated remaining fragment of verse:

> I went to Frankfort and got drunk
> With that most learned Professor Brunck;
> I went to Wortz and got more drunken
> With that more learned Professor Ruhnken.—*Ed.*

When he lived in Essex Court, Temple, he would shut himself up for three or four days together, admitting no visitors to his chambers. One morning I went to call upon him there; and having inquired at his barber's close by "if Mr. Porson was at home," was answered "Yes, but he has seen no one for two days." I, however, proceeded to his chambers, and knocked at the door more than once. He would not open it, and I came down stairs. As I was re-crossing the court, Porson, who had perceived that *I* was the visitor, opened the window, and stopped me. He was then busy about the Grenville Homer, for which he collated the Harleian Ms. of the Odyssey. His labours on that work were rewarded with 50*l*. and a large-paper copy. I thought the payment too small, but Burney considered it as sufficient.

Postlethwaite* having come to London to attend the Westminster Examination, Porson called upon him, when the following dialogue (which I wrote down from Porson's dictation) took place between them.—*Porson*. " I am come, sir, to inform you that my fellowship will become vacant in a few weeks, in order that you may appoint my successor." *Postle*. " But, Mr. Porson, you do not mean to leave us? "— *Porson*. " It is not I who leave you, but you who dismiss me. You have done me every injury in your power. But I am not come to complain or expostulate." *Postle*. " I did not know, Mr. Porson, you were so resolved."—

* Master of Trinity College, Cambridge.

Porson. " You could not conceive, sir, that I should have applied for a lay-fellowship to the detriment of some more scrupulous man, if it had been my intention to take orders."

In 1792, Postlethwaite wrote a letter to Porson, informing him that the Greek Professorship at Cambridge had fallen vacant. Here is an exact copy of Porson's answer:

" SIR,—When I first received the favour of your letter, I must own that I felt rather vexation and chagrin than hope and satisfaction. I had looked upon myself so completely in the light of an outcast from Alma Mater, that I had made up my mind to have no farther connexion with the place. The prospect you held out to me gave me more uneasiness than pleasure. When I was younger than I now am, and my disposition more sanguine than it is at present, I was in daily expectation of Mr. Cooke's resignation, and I flattered myself with the hope of succeeding to the honour he was going to quit. As hope and ambition are great castle-builders, I had laid a scheme, partly, as I was willing to think, for the joint credit, partly for the mutual advantage, of myself and the University. I had projected a plan of reading lectures, and I persuaded myself that I should easily obtain a grace permitting me to exact a certain sum from every person who attended. But seven years' waiting will tire out the most patient temper; and all my ambition of this sort was long ago laid asleep. The sudden news of the vacant professorship put me in mind of poor

Jacob, who, having served seven years in hopes of being rewarded with Rachel, awoke, and behold it was Leah!

" Such, sir, I confess, were the first ideas that took possession of my mind. But after a little reflection, I resolved to refer a matter of this importance to my friends. This circumstance has caused the delay, for which I ought before now to have apologised. My friends unanimously exhorted me to embrace the good fortune which they conceived to be within my grasp. Their advice, therefore, joined to the expectation I had entertained of doing some small good by my exertions in the employment, together with the pardonable vanity which the honour annexed to the office inspired, determined me: and I was on the point of troubling you, sir, and the other electors with notice of my intentions to profess myself a candidate, when an objection, which had escaped me in the hurry of my thoughts, now occurred to my recollection.

" The same reason which hindered me from keeping my fellowship by the method you obligingly pointed out to me, would, I am greatly afraid, prevent me from being Greek Professor. Whatever concern this may give me for myself, it gives me none for the public. I trust there are at least twenty or thirty in the University equally able and willing to undertake the office; possessed, many, of talents superior to mine, and all of a more complying conscience. This I speak upon the supposition that the next Greek Professor will be compelled to read lectures: but if the place remains a sinecure, the number of qualified persons will be greatly increased. And though it were even granted, that my industry and attention might possibly produce some benefit to the interests of learning and the credit of the University, that trifling gain would be as much exceeded by keeping the Professorship a sinecure, and bestowing it on a sound believer, as temporal considerations are outweighed by spiritual. Having only a strong persuasion, not an absolute certainty, that such a subscription is required of the Professor elect,— if I am mistaken, I hereby offer myself as a candidate; but if I am right in my opinion, I shall beg of you to order my name to be erased from the boards, and I shall esteem it a favour conferred on, sir,

" Your obliged humble servant,

" R. PORSON.

" Essex Court, Temple, 6th October 1792."

When he was first elected Greek Professor,* he assured me that he intended to give public lectures in that capacity. I afterwards asked him why he had not given them. He replied, " Because I have thought better on it: whatever originality my lectures might have had, people would have cried out, *We knew all this before*."

I was with him one day when he bought Drakenborch's Livy; and I said, " Do you

---

* In 1793, by an unanimous vote of the seven electors.—According to the printed accounts of Porson, he was prevented from giving lectures by the want of rooms for that purpose.

mean to read through all the notes in these seven quarto volumes? " " I buy it at least," he answered, " in the hope of doing so some time or other: there is no doubt a deal of valuable information to be found in the notes; and I shall endeavour to collect that information. Indeed, I should like to publish a volume of the curious things which I have gathered in the course of my studies; but people would only say of it, *We knew all this before*."

Porson had no very high opinion of Parr, and could not ensure his metaphysics. One evening, Parr was beginning a regular harangue on the origin of evil, when Porson stopped him short by asking " what was the use of it? "—Porson, who shrunk on all occasions from praise of himself, was only annoyed by the eulogies which Parr lavished upon him in print. When Parr published the *Remarks on Combe's Statement*, in which Porson is termed " a giant in literature," &c., Porson said, " How should Dr. Parr be able to take the measure of a giant? "

Parr was evidently afraid of Porson,—of his intellectual powers. I might say too that Horne Tooke had a dread of Porson; but it was only the dread of being insulted by some rude speech from Porson in his drunkenness. Porson thought highly both of Tooke's natural endowments and of his acquirements. " I have learned many valuable things from Tooke," was what he frequently said; " yet I don't always believe Tooke's assertions."

I believe that Burney was indebted to Porson

for many of those remarks on various niceties of Greek which he has given as his own in different publications. Porson once said to me, " A certain gentleman " (evidently meaning Burney) " has just been with me; and he brought me a long string of questions, every one of which I answered off-hand. Really, before people become schoolmasters, they ought to get up their Greek thoroughly, for they never learn any thing more of it afterwards."—I one day asked Burney for his opinion of Porson as a scholar. Burney replied, " I think my friend Dick's acquaintance with the Greek dramatists quite marvellous; but he was just as well acquainted with them at the age of thirty as he is now: he has not improved in Greek since he added brandy-and-water to his potations, and took to novel-reading." Porson would sometimes read nothing but novels for a fortnight together.

Cleaver Banks once invited Porson (about a year before his death) to dine with him at an hotel at the west end of London; but the dinner passed away without the expected guest having made his appearance. Afterwards, on Banks's asking him why he had not kept his engagement, Porson replied (without entering into further particulars) that " he *had* come ": and Banks could only conjecture, that the waiters, seeing Porson's shabby dress, and not knowing who he was, had offered him some insult, which had made him indignantly return home.

" I hear," said I to Porson, " that you are to

dine to-day at Holland House." "Who told you so?" asked he.—I replied, "Mackintosh." "But I certainly shall not go," continued Porson: "they invite me merely out of curiosity; and, after they have satisfied it, they would like to kick me down stairs." I then informed him that Fox was coming from St. Anne's Hill to Holland House for the express purpose of being introduced to him: but he persisted in his resolution; and dined quietly with Rogers and myself at Rogers's chambers in the Temple. Many years afterwards, Lord Holland mentioned to Rogers that his uncle (Fox) had been greatly disappointed at not meeting Porson on that occasion.

One day Porson took up in my room a nicely bound copy of the *Polycraticon* (by John of Salisbury), and having dipped into it, said, "I must read this through"; so he carried it off. About a month had elapsed, when calling at his chambers, I happened to see my beautiful book lying on the floor and covered with dust. This vexed me; and I mentioned the circumstance to Mr. Maltby (an elder brother of the Bishop of Durham), who repeated to Porson what I had said. A day or two after, I dined with Porson at Rogers's: he swallowed a good deal of wine; and then began in a loud voice an indirect attack on me,—"There are certain people who complain that I use their books roughly," &c. &c. I was quite silent; and when he found that I would not take any notice of his tirade, he dropped the subject.

When Porson was told that Pretyman* had been left a large estate by a person who had seen him only once, he said, " It would not have happened, if the person had seen him twice."

Meeting me one day at a booksale, Porson said, " That * * * the Bishop of Lincoln (Tomline) has just passed me in the street, and he shrunk from my eye like a wild animal. What do you think he has had the impudence to assert? Not long ago, he came to me, and, after informing me that Lord Elgin was appointed ambassador to the Porte, he asked me if I knew any one who was competent to examine the Greek manuscripts at Constantinople: I replied, that I did not: and he now tells every body that I refused the proposal of government *that I should go there to examine those manuscripts!* " —I do not believe that Porson would have gone to Constantinople, if he had had the offer. He hated moving; and would not even accompany me to Paris.

When Porson first met Perry after the fire in the house of the latter at Merton, he immediately inquired " if any lives had been lost? " Perry replied " No." " Well," said Porson, " then I shall not complain, though I have lost the labours of my life." His transcript of the Cambridge *Photius*, which was burnt in that fire, he afterwards replaced by patiently making

---

* Then Bishop of Lincoln. A valuable estate was bequeathed to him by Marmaduke Tomline (a gentleman with whom he had no relationship or connection), on condition of his taking the name of Tomline.

a second transcript; but his numerous notes on Aristophanes, which had also been consumed, were irrecoverably gone.

For the scholarship of that amiable man Bishop Burgess he felt a contempt which he was unable to conceal. He was once on a visit at Oxford, in company with Cleaver Banks, where, during a supper-party, he gave great offence by talking of Burgess with any thing but respect. At the same supper-party, too, he offended Professor Holmes:* taking up an oyster which happened to be gaping, he exclaimed, *Quid dignum tanto feret hic* professor *hiatu?*† (substituting " professor " for " *promissor* ").

A gentleman who had heard that Bentley was born in the north, said to Porson, " Wasn't he a Scotchman? "—" No, sir," replied Porson; " Bentley was a great Greek scholar."

He said, " Pearson would have been a first-rate critic in Greek, if he had not muddled his brains with divinity."

His favourite authors in Greek (as, I believe, every body knows) were the tragedians and Aristophanes; he had them almost by heart.

He confessed to me and the present Bishop of Durham (Maltby), that he knew comparatively little of Thucydides,—that, when he read him, he was obliged to mark with a pencil, in almost every page, passages which he did not understand.

He dabbled a good deal in Galen.

He cared less about Lucian than, considering

---

* The then Professor of Poetry.
† Horace, *Ars Poet.* 138.

the subjects of that writer, you might suppose; the fact was, he did not relish such late Greek.

He sent Thomas Taylor* several emendations

* With that remarkable person, Thomas Taylor, I was well acquainted. In Greek verbal scholarship he was no doubt very deficient (he was entirely self-taught); but in a knowledge of the *matter* of Plato, of Aristotle, of the commentators on Aristotle (themselves a library), of Proclus, of Plotinus, &c., he has never, I presume, been equalled by any Englishman. That he endeavoured to carry into practice the precepts of the ancient philosophers is sufficiently notorious: that he did so to the last hour of his existence I myself had a proof: the day before he died, I went to see him; and to my inquiry " how he was ? " he answered, " I have passed a dreadful night of pain,—*but you remember what Posidonius said to Pompey* " (about pain being no evil).

Chalmers, in his *Biog. Dict.*, expresses his regret that he can tell so little about Floyer Sydenham, the excellent translator of Plato, and remarks that he " deserves a fuller account." I give the following particulars concerning him on the authority of Taylor, who when a young man was intimate with Sydenham, and who, let me add, had a scrupulous regard to truth in whatever he stated.— Sydenham was originally a clergyman with a living of about 800*l.* per annum; but, having fallen in love with a young lady whose father objected to his addresses because he was in the church, he threw up his living, and had recourse to the law as a profession. After all, it appears, he did not marry the fair one for whose sake he had sacrificed so much. Having made no progress at the bar, he entered the naval service, went abroad, endured many hardships, and finally worked his way back to England as a common sailor. He was far from young when he first applied himself to the study of Plato. During his later years Taylor became acquainted with him. On their first meeting, Sydenham shook Taylor cordially by the hand, and said he reckoned himself truly fortunate in having at last met with a real Platonist,—deeply regretting his own want of familiarity with Proclus and Plotinus. He at that time lodged at the house of a statuary in the Strand. He was in very distressed circumstances; and regularly received two guineas a month from Harris (the author of *Hermes*). He used to dine at a neighbouring eating-house, where he had run up a bill of 40*l.* This debt, as well as several other debts, he was unable to pay; and his acquaintances refused to discharge his bills, though they consented to maintain him during his abode in the Fleet-prison, where he was about to be confined. The night preceding the day on which he was to be carried to gaol he was found dead,—having undoubtedly (as Taylor asserted) put an end to his existence. For some time before his death he had been partially insane: as he went up and down stairs, he fancied turkeys were gobbling at him, &c.

of Plato's text for his translation of that philosopher; but Taylor, from his ignorance of the Greek language, was unable to use them.

He read a vast number of French works, and used to say, " If I had a son, I should endeavour to make him familiar with French and English authors, rather than with the classics. Greek and Latin are only luxuries."

He delighted in Milton. " If I live," he exclaimed, " I will write an essay to show the world how unjustly Milton has been treated by Johnson."—(George Steevens told me that Johnson said to him, " In my *Life of Milton* I have spoken of the *Paradise Lost*, not so much from my own conviction of its merit, as in compliance with the taste of the multitude."—A very old gentleman, who had known Johnson intimately, assured me that the bent of his mind was decidedly towards scepticism; that he was literally afraid to examine his own thoughts on religious matters; and that hence partly arose his hatred of Hume and other such writers.—Dr. Gosset (as he himself told me) once dined with Johnson and a few others at Dr. Musgrave's (the editor of *Euripides*). During dinner, while Musgrave was holding forth very agreeably on some subject, Johnson suddenly interrupted him with, " Sir, you talk like a fool." A dead silence ensued; and Johnson, perceiving that his rude speech had occasioned it, turned to Musgrave, and said, " Sir, I fear I have hurt your feelings." " Dr. Johnson," replied Musgrave, " I feel only for *you*."—I have often heard Mrs. Carter* say, that, rude as Johnson might occasionally be to others, both male and female, he had invariably treated her with gentleness and kindness. She perfectly adored his memory; and she used to read his *Tour to the Hebrides* once every year, thinking it, as I do, one of his best works.)

Porson was passionately fond of Swift's *Tale of a Tub*, and whenever he saw a copy of it on a stall, he would purchase it. He could repeat by heart a quantity of Swift's verses.

His admiration of Pope was extreme. I have seen the tears roll down his cheeks while he was repeating Pope's lines *To the Earl of Oxford, prefixed to Parnell's Poems* (and, indeed, I have seen him weep, while repeating other favourite passages,—the chorus in the *Hercules Furens* of Euripides, ῾Α νεότας μοι φίλον ἄχθος, &c.). He thought Pope's Homer, in the finest passages of the poem, superior to Cowper's. One forenoon, while he was going over Pope's villa at Twickenham, in company with Rogers and myself, he said, " Oh, how I should like to pass the remainder of my days in a house which was the abode of a man so deservedly celebrated! "

He was fond of Foote's plays, and would often recite scenes from them.

Junius was one of his favourite authors; he had many passages of him by heart.

He greatly admired and used often to repeat

* Mrs. Elizabeth Carter, translator of Epictetus.—*Ed.*

the following passage from the Preface to Middleton's *Free Inquiry:*

" I persuade myself that the life and faculties of man, at the best but short and limited, cannot be employed more rationally or laudably than in the search of knowledge; and especially of that sort which relates to our duty and conduces to our happiness. In these inquiries, therefore, wherever I perceive any glimmering of truth before me, I readily pursue and endeavour to trace it to its source, without any reserve or caution of pushing the discovery too far, or opening too great a glare of it to the public. I look upon the discovery of any thing which is true as a valuable acquisition to society; which cannot possibly hurt or obstruct the good effect of any other truth whatsoever; for they all partake of one common essence, and necessarily coincide with each other; and like the drops of rain, which fall separately into the river, mix themselves at once with the stream, and strengthen the general current."

He liked Moore's *Fables for the Female Sex*, and I have heard him repeat the one which is entitled " The Female Seducers."*

At a booksale, the auctioneer having put up Wilkes's edition of *Theophrastus*, and praised it highly, Porson exclaimed, " Pooh, pooh, it is

* This now-forgotten poem was once very popular. Speaking of Dr. Mudge, " I remember," said Northcote, " his once reading Moore's fable of *The Female Seducers* with such feeling and sweetness that every one was delighted, and Dr. Mudge himself was so much affected that he burst into tears in the middle of it." Hazlitt's *Conversations of Northcote*, p. 89. At present Moore is only recollected as the author of *The Gamester*.

like its editor,—of no character."—(I was very intimate with Wilkes. He felt excessively angry at the account given of him in Gibbon's "Journal"—in the quarto edition—and said to me that "Gibbon must have been drunk when he wrote that passage." The fact is, Lord Sheffield printed in the quarto edition only *part of what Gibbon had written about Wilkes*: if the whole of it had appeared there, as it afterwards did in the octavo edition, I have no doubt that Wilkes would have called out Lord Sheffield.)

On returning from a visit to the Lakes, I told Porson that Southey had said to me, " My *Madoc* has brought me in a mere trifle; but that poem will be a valuable possession to my family." Porson answered, " *Madoc* will be read,—when Homer and Virgil are forgotten " (a *bon-mot* which reached Lord Byron, and which his lordship spoilt*).

He disliked reading folios, " because," said he, " we meet with so few mile-stones "(*i.e.* we have such long intervals between the turning over of the leaves).

When asked why he had written so little, Porson replied, " I doubt if I could produce any original work which would command the attention of posterity. I can be known only by my notes: and I am quite satisfied if, three hundred years hence, it shall be said that ' one

* " Joan of Arc was marvellous enough; but Thalaba was one of those poems ' which,' in the words of Porson, ' will be read when Homer and Virgil are forgotten,—but—*not till then.*' " Note on *English Bards and Scotch Reviewers*.

Porson lived towards the close of the eighteenth century, who did a good deal for the text of Euripides.' "

Porson thought meanly of the medical science, and hated consulting physicians. He once said to me, " I have been staying with Dr. Davy at Cambridge: I was unwell, and he prevailed upon me to call in a physician, who took my money, and did me no good."

During the earlier part of our acquaintance, I have heard him boast that he had not the slightest dread of death,—declaring that he despised *fabulæ aniles*, and quoting Epicharmus (from Cicero*), &c. He was once holding forth in this strain, when Dr. Babington said to him, " Let me tell you, Porson, that I have known several persons who, though, when in perfect health, they talked as you do now, were yet dreadfully alarmed when death was really near them."

A man of such habits as Porson was little fitted for the office of Librarian to the London Institution. He was very irregular in his attendance there; he never troubled himself about the purchase of books which ought to have been added to the library; and he would frequently come home dead-drunk long after midnight. I have good reason to believe that, had he lived, he would have been requested to give up the office,—in other words, he would have been dismissed. I once read a letter which he received from the Directors of the

* *Tusc.* i. 8.

Institution, and which contained, among other severe things, this cutting remark,—" We only know that you are our Librarian by seeing your name attached to the receipts for your salary." As Librarian to the Institution, he had 200*l.* a-year, apartments rent-free, and the use of a servant. Yet he was eternally railing at the Directors, calling them " mercantile and mean beyond merchandize and meanness."

During the two last years of his life I could perceive that he was not a little shaken; and it is really wonderful, when we consider his drinking, and his total disregard of hours, that he lived so long as he did. He told me that he had had an affection of the lungs from his boyhood.

Rogers' anecdotes (continued):—

Lord Seaforth, who was born deaf and dumb, was to dine one day with Lord Melville. Just before the time of the company's arrival, Lady Melville sent into the drawing-room a lady of her acquaintance, who could talk with her fingers to dumb people, that she might receive Lord Seaforth. Presently Lord Guilford entered the room; and the lady, taking him for Lord Seaforth, began to ply her fingers very nimbly: Lord Guilford did the same; and they had been carrying on a conversation in this manner for about ten minutes, when Lady Melville joined them. Her female friend immediately said, " Well, I have been talking away to this dumb man."—" Dumb! " cried Lord Guilford; " bless me, I thought *you* were dumb."—I told this story (which is perfectly true) to Matthews; and he said that he could make excellent use of it at one of his evening-entertainments: but I know not if he ever did.

I can discover from a poet's versification whether or not he has an ear for music. Shakespeare's, Milton's, Dryden's, and Gray's prove to me that they had it; Pope's that he had it not:—indeed, with respect to Shakespeare, the passage in *The Merchant of Venice** would be enough to settle the question. To instance poets of the present day;—from Bowles's and Moore's versification, I should know that they had fine ears for music; from Southey's, Wordsworth's, and Byron's, that they had no ears for it.

To any one who has reached a very advanced age, a walk through the streets of London is like a walk in a cemetery. How many houses do I pass, now inhabited by strangers, in which I used to spend such happy hours with those who have long been dead and gone!

A friend of mine in Portland Place has a wife who inflicts upon him every season two or three immense evening parties. At one of those

* Act v. sc. 1.

parties he was standing in a very forlorn condition, leaning against the chimney-piece, when a gentleman, coming up to him, said, "Sir, as neither of us is acquainted with any of the people here, I think we had best go home."

One of the books which I never tire reading is *Mémoires sur la vie de Jean Racine*, by his son.

When I was living in the Temple, the chimneys of one of my neighbours were to be swept. Up went two boys; and at the end of an hour they had not come down again. Two other boys were then sent up; and up they remained also. The master of the boys was now summoned, who, on his arrival, exclaimed, "Oh, the idle little rascals! they are playing at all-fours on the top of the chimney." And, to be sure, there they were, trumping it away at their ease. I suppose *spades* were their favourite cards.

How little Crowe* is known even to persons who are fond of poetry! Yet his *Lewesdon Hill* is full of noble passages.

Crowe was an intimate friend of mine.— When I was travelling in Italy, I made two authors my constant study for versification,— Milton and Crowe.

* William Crowe (1745–1829), Public Orator at the University of Oxford.—*Ed.*

Most people are ever on the watch to find fault with their children, and are afraid of *praising* them for fear of *spoiling* them. Now, I am sure that nothing has a better effect on children than *praise*. I had a proof of this in Moore's daughter: he used always to be saying to her, " What a *good* little girl! " and she continued to grow more and more good, till she became too good for this world and died.

Did ever poet, dramatist, or novel-writer, devise a more effective incident than the falling of the rug in Molly Seagrim's bedroom? Can any thing be more happily ludicrous, when we consider how the actors in that scene are connected with each other? It probably suggested to Sheridan the falling of the screen in *The School for Scandal.**

Neither Moore nor myself had ever seen Byron when it was settled that he should dine at my house to meet Moore; nor was he known by sight to Campbell, who, happening to call upon me that morning, consented to join the party. I thought it best that I alone should be in the drawing-room when Byron entered it; and Moore and Campbell accordingly withdrew. Soon after his arrival, they returned; and I introduced them to him severally, naming

* No doubt it did; as the Jones and Blifil of the same novel suggested to him Charles and Joseph Surface.

them as Adam named the beasts. When we sat down to dinner, I asked Byron if he would take soup? "No; he never took soup."— Would he take some fish? "No; he never took fish."—Presently I asked if he would eat some mutton? "No; he never ate mutton."— I then asked if he would take a glass of wine? "No; he never tasted wine."—It was now necessary to inquire what he *did* eat and drink; and the answer was, "Nothing but hard biscuits and soda-water." Unfortunately, neither hard biscuits nor soda-water were at hand; and he dined upon potatoes bruised down on his plate and drenched with vinegar.—My guests stayed till very late, discussing the merits of Walter Scott and Joanna Baillie.—Some days after, meeting Hobhouse, I said to him, "How long will Lord Byron persevere in his present diet?" He replied, "Just as long as you continue to notice it."—I did not then know, what I now know to be a fact,—that Byron, after leaving my house, had gone to a Club in St. James's Street, and eaten a hearty meat-supper.

Byron sent me *Childe Harold* in the printed sheets before it was published; and I read it to my sister. "This," I said, "in spite of all its beauty, will never please the public: they will dislike the querulous repining tone that pervades it, and the dissolute character of the hero." But I quickly found that I was mistaken. The genius which the poem exhibited, the youth, the rank of the author, his romantic wanderings in Greece,—these combined to make the world stark mad about *Childe Harold* and Byron. I knew two old maids in Buckinghamshire who used to cry over the passage about Harold's "laughing dames" that "long had fed his youthful appetite,"* &c.

After Byron had become the *rage*, I was frequently amused at the manœuvres of certain noble ladies to get acquainted with him by means of me: for instance, I would receive a note from Lady —— requesting the pleasure of my company on a particular evening, with a postscript, "Pray, could you not contrive to bring Lord Byron with you?"—Once, at a great party given by Lady Jersey, Mrs. Sheridan ran up to me and said, "Do, as a favour, try if you can place Lord Byron beside me at supper."

Byron had prodigious facility of composition. He was fond of suppers; and used often to sup at my house and eat heartily (for he had then given up the hard biscuit and soda-water diet): after going home, he would throw off sixty or eighty verses, which he would send to press next morning.

He one evening took me to the green-room of Drury Lane Theatre, where I was much entertained. When the play began, I went round to the front of the house, and desired the box-keeper to show me into Lord Byron's box. I had been there about a minute, thinking myself quite alone, when suddenly Byron and Miss Boyce (the actress) emerged from a dark corner.

* Canto i. st. 11.

In those days at least, Byron had no readiness of reply in conversation. If you happened to let fall any observation which offended him, he would say nothing at the time; but the offence would lie rankling in his mind; and perhaps a fortnight after, he would suddenly come out with some very cutting remarks upon you, giving them as his deliberate opinions, the results of his experience of your character.

Several women were in love with Byron, but none so violently as Lady Caroline Lamb. She absolutely besieged him. He showed me the first letter he received from her; in which she assured him that, if he was in any want of money, " all her jewels were at his service." They frequently had quarrels; and more than once, on coming home, I have found Lady C. walking in the garden,* and waiting for me, to beg that I would reconcile them.—When she met Byron at a party, she would always, if possible, return home from it in *his* carriage, and accompanied by *him:* I recollect particularly their returning to town together from Holland House.—But such was the insanity of her passion for Byron, that sometimes, when not invited to a party where he was to be, she would wait for him in the street till it was over! One night, after a great party at Devonshire House, to which Lady Caroline had not been invited, I saw her,—yes, saw her,—talking to Byron, with half of her body thrust into the carriage which he had just entered. In spite of all this absurdity,

* Behind Mr. Rogers's house, in St. James's Place.

my firm belief is that there was nothing criminal between them.

Byron at last was sick of her. When their intimacy was at an end, and while she was living in the country, she burned, very solemnly, on a sort of funeral pile, *transcripts* of all the letters which she had received from Byron, and *a copy* of a miniature (his portrait) which he had presented to her; several girls from the neighbourhood, whom she had dressed in white garments, dancing round the pile, and singing a song which she had written for the occasion, " Burn, fire, burn," &c.—She was mad; and her family allowed her to do whatever she chose.

Latterly, I believe, Byron never dined with Lady B.; for it was one of his fancies (or affectations) that " he could not endure to see women eat." I recollect that he once refused to meet Madame de Staël at my house *at dinner*, but came in the evening; and when I have asked him to dinner without mentioning what company I was to have, he would write me a note to inquire " if I had invited any women."

Wilkes's daughter may have had a right to burn her father's *Memoirs;** but Moore, I conceive, was not justified in giving his consent to the burning of Byron's: when Byron told him that he might " do whatever he pleased with them," Byron certainly never contemplated their being burned. If Moore had made me his

* " Wilkes said to me, ' I have written my *Memoirs*, and they are to be published by Peter Elmsley, after my *ascension*.' They were burnt by his daughter."—*Maltby*.

confidant in the business, I should have pro-
tested warmly against the destruction of the
Memoirs: but he chose Luttrell, probably because
he thought him the more fashionable man; and
Luttrell, who cared nothing about the matter,
readily voted that they should be put into the
fire.—There were, I understand, some gross
things in that manuscript; but I read only a
portion of it, and did not light upon them. I
remember that it contained this anecdote:—on
his marriage-night, Byron suddenly started out
of his first sleep: a taper, which burned in the
room, was casting a ruddy glare through the
crimson curtains of the bed; and he could not
help exclaiming, in a voice so loud that he
wakened Lady B., " Good God, I am surely
in hell! "

My latest intercourse with Byron was in Italy.
We travelled some time together; and, if there
was any scenery particularly well worth seeing,
he generally contrived that we should pass
through it in the dark.

As we were crossing the Apennines, he told
me that he had left an order in his will that
Allegra, the child who soon after died, his
daughter by Miss C.,* should never be taught
the English language.—You know that Allegra
was buried at Harrow: but probably you have
not heard that the body was sent over to England
in *two* packages, that no one might suspect what
it was.

About the same time he said,—being at last

* Clairmont.—*Ed.*

assured that the celebrated critique on his early poems in *The Edinburgh Review* was written by Lord Brougham,—" If ever I return to England, Brougham shall hear from me." He added, " That critique cost me three bottles of claret " (to raise his spirits after reading it).*

One day, during dinner, at Pisa,† when Shelley and Trelawney were with us, Byron chose to run down Shakespeare (for whom he, like Sheridan, either had, or pretended to have, little admiration). I said nothing. But Shelley immediately took up the defence of the great

* Wordsworth was spending an evening at Charles Lamb's, when he first saw the said critique, which had just appeared. He read it through, and remarked that " though Byron's verses were probably poor enough, yet such an attack was abominable,—that a young nobleman, who took to poetry, deserved to be encouraged, not ridiculed." Perhaps if this had been made known to Byron, he would not have spoken of Wordsworth as he has done.—Many years ago Wordsworth gave me the following account, which I noted down at the time. " Lord Byron's hatred towards me originated thus. There was a woman in distressed circumstances at Bristol, who wrote a volume of poems, which she wished to publish and dedicate to me. She had formed an idea that, if she became a poetess, her fortune would be made. I endeavoured to dissuade her from indulging such vain expectations, and advised her to turn her attention to something else. I represented to her how little chance there was that her poems, though really evincing a good deal of talent, would make any impression on the public; and I observed that, in our day, two persons only (whom I did not name) had succeeded in making money by their poetry, adding that in the writings of the one (Sir Walter Scott) there was little poetic feeling, and that in those of the other (Lord Byron) it was perverted. Mr. Rogers told me that when he was travelling with Lord Byron in Italy, his lordship confessed that the hatred he bore me arose from the remark about his poetry which I had made to that woman, and which some good-natured friend had repeated to him."

† In Moore's *Life* of Byron no mention is made of Mr. Rogers having been Byron's guest at Pisa.—In Medwin's *Angler in Wales*, i. 25, is an account,—exaggerated perhaps, but doubtless substantially true,—of Byron's *wicked* behaviour to Mr. Rogers at the Casa Lanfranchi.

poet, and conducted it in his usual meek yet resolute manner, unmoved by the rude things with which Byron interrupted him,—" Oh, that's very well *for an atheist*," &c. (Before meeting Shelley in Italy, I had seen him only once. It was at my own house in St. James's Place, where he called upon me,—introducing himself,—to request the loan of some money which he wished to present to Leigh Hunt; and he offered me a bond for it. Having numerous claims upon me at that time, I was obliged to refuse the loan. Both in appearance and in manners Shelley was the perfect gentleman.)—That same day, after dinner, I walked in the garden with Byron. At the window of a neighbouring house was a young woman holding a child in her arms. Byron nodded to her with a smile, and then, turning to me, said, " That child is mine." In the evening, we (*i.e.* Byron, Shelley, Trelawney, and I) rode out from Pisa to a farm (a *podere*); and there a pistol was put into my hand for shooting at a mark (a favourite amusement of Byron); but I declined trying my skill with it. The farm-keeper's daughter was very pretty, and had her arms covered with bracelets, the gift of Byron, who did not fail to let me know that she was one of his many loves.

I went with him to see the Campo Santo at Pisa. It was shown to us by a man who had two handsome daughters. Byron told me that he had in vain paid his addresses to the elder daughter, but that he was on the most intimate terms with the other. Probably there was not one syllable of truth in all this; for he always had the weakness of wishing to be thought much worse than he really was.

Byron, like Sir Walter Scott,* was without any feeling for the fine arts. He accompanied me to the Pitti Palace at Florence; but soon growing tired of looking at the pictures, he sat down in a corner; and when I called out to him, " What a noble Andrea del Sarto! " the only answer I received was his muttering a passage from *The Vicar of Wakefield*,—" Upon asking how he had been taught the art of a cognoscente so very suddenly," &c.† (When he and Hobhouse were standing before the Parthenon, the latter said, " Well, this is surely very grand." Byron replied, " Very like the Mansion-House.")

At this time we generally had a regular quarrel every night; and he would abuse me through thick and thin, raking up all the stories he had heard which he thought most likely to mortify me,—how I had behaved with great cruelty to Murphy, refusing to assist him in his distress, &c. &c. But next morning he would shake me

* " During Scott's first visit to Paris, I walked with him (and Richard Sharp) through the Louvre, and pointed out for his particular notice the St. Jerome of Domenichino, and some other chefs-d'œuvre. Scott merely glanced at them, and passed on, saying, ' I really have not time to examine them.' "—*Maltby*.

† " Upon asking how he had been taught the art of a cognoscente so very suddenly, he assured me that nothing was more easy. The whole secret consisted in a strict adherence to two rules; the one, always to observe the picture might have been better if the painter had taken more pains; and the other, to praise the works of Pietro Perugino." Chap. xx. Compare Byron's own account of this visit to the Pitti Palace in his *Life* by Moore, vol. v. 279.

kindly by both hands; and we were excellent friends again.

When I parted from him in Italy (never to meet him more), a good many persons were looking on, anxious to catch a glimpse of " the famous lord."

Campbell used to say that the lines which first convinced him that Byron was a true poet were these;

" Yet are thy skies as blue, thy crags as wild;
 Sweet are thy groves, and verdant are thy fields,
  Thine olive ripe as when Minerva smil'd,
  And still his honied wealth Hymettus yields;
  There the blithe bee his fragrant fortress builds,
  The free-born wanderer of thy mountain-air;
  Apollo still thy long, long summer gilds,
  Still in his beam Mendeli's marbles glare;
 Art, Glory, Freedom fail, but Nature still is fair.

  Where'er we tread, 'tis haunted, holy ground,
  No earth of thine is lost in vulgar mould,
  But one vast realm of wonder spreads around,
  And all the Muse's tales seem truly told,
  Till the sense aches with gazing to behold

The scenes our earliest dreams have
    dwelt upon:
Each hill and dale, each deepening glen
    and wold
Defies the power which crush'd thy temples
    gone:
Age shakes Athenæ's tower, but spares gray
    Marathon."*

For my own part, I think that this passage is
perhaps the best that Byron ever wrote;

" To sit on rocks, to muse o'er flood and fell,
To slowly trace the forest's shady scene,
    Where things that own not man's
    dominion dwell,
And mortal foot hath ne'er or rarely been;
To climb the trackless mountain all unseen,
With the wild flock that never needs a fold;
Alone o'er steeps and foaming falls to lean;
This is not solitude; 'tis but to hold
Converse with Nature's charms, and view
    her stores unroll'd.

But midst the crowd, the hum, the shock
    of men,
To hear, to see, to feel, and to possess,
And roam along, the world's tir'd denizen,
With none who bless us, none whom we
    can bless;
Minions of splendour shrinking from
    distress!

* *Childe Harold*, c. ii. st. 87, 88.

None that, with kindred consciousness
    endued,
If we were not, would seem to smile the less,
Of all that flatter'd, follow'd, sought, and
    sued;
This is to be alone; this, this is solitude."*

The lines in the third canto of *Childe Harold*
about the ball given by the Duchess of Richmond
at Brussels, the night before the battle of
Waterloo, &c. are very striking. The Duchess
told me that she had a list of her company, and
that, after the battle, she added " dead " to the
names of those who had fallen,—the number
being fearful.

Mrs. Barbauld once observed to me that *she*
thought Byron wrote best when he wrote about
the *sea* or *swimming*.

There is a great deal of incorrect and hasty
writing in Byron's works; but it is overlooked
in this age of hasty readers.   For instance,

" I stood in Venice, on the Bridge of Sighs,
    A palace and a prison *on each hand*."†

He meant to say, that on one hand was a palace,
on the other a prison.—And what think you of—

" And dashest him again to earth:—there let
    him *lay* "?‡

* *Childe Harold*, c. ii. st. 25, 26.
† Id. c. iv. st. 1.
‡ Id. c. iv. st. 180.—A lady resident in Aberdeen told me that she
used to sit in a pew of St. Paul's Chapel in that town, next to Mrs.
(*continued on next page*)

Mr. ——'s house, the ——, is very splendid; it contains a quantity of or-molu. Now, I like to have a kettle in my bed-room, to heat a little water if necessary: but I can't get a kettle at the ——, though there is a quantity of or-molu. Lady —— says, that when she is at the ——, she is obliged to have her clothes unpacked three times a day; for there are no chests-of-drawers, though there is a quantity of or-molu.

The letters I receive from people, of both sexes (people whom I never heard of), asking me for money, either as a gift or as a loan, are really

(continued from previous page)
Byron's; and that one Sunday she observed the poet (then about seven or eight years old) amusing himself by disturbing his mother's devotions: he every now and then gently pricked with a pin the large round arms of Mrs. Byron, which were covered with white kid gloves.—Professor Stuart, of the Marischal College, Aberdeen, mentioned to me the following proof of Lord Byron's fondness for his mother. *Georgy*, and some other little boys, were one day allowed, much to their delight, to assist at a gathering of apples in the Professor's garden, and were rewarded for their labour with some of the fruit. *Georgy*, having received his portion of apples, immediately disappeared; and, on his return, after half-an-hour's absence, to the inquiry where he had been, he replied that he had been " carrying some apples to his poor dear mother."

At the house of the Rev. W. Harness I remember hearing Moore remark, that he thought the natural bent of Byron's genius was to satirical and burlesque poetry: on which Mr. Harness related what follows. One day at Harrow Byron was running after his school-fellow Tattersal (the *Davus* of the *Hours of Idleness*); but not being able to overtake him, and wishing to stop him, he bawled out this extemporaneous couplet,—

> " Bold *Robert Speer* was *Bony's* bad precursor;
> *Bob* was a bloody dog, but *Bonapart's a worser*."

Moore immediately wrote the lines down, with the intention of inserting them in his *Life of Byron*, which he was then preparing; but they do not appear in that work.

innumerable. Here's one from a student at Durham, requesting me to lend him 90*l.* (how modest to stop short of the hundred!). I lately had a begging epistle from a lady, who assured me that she used formerly to take evening walks with me in the Park: of course I did not answer it; and a day or two after, I had a second letter from her, beginning " Unkind one! "

Uvedale Price once chose to stay so long at my house, that I began to think he would never go away; so I one day ingeniously said to him, " You must not leave me *before the end of next week;* if you insist on going after that, you may; but certainly not before." And at the end of the week he *did* go. He was a most elegant letter-writer; and his son had some intention of collecting and publishing his correspondence.

Not long before Mrs. Inchbald died, I met her walking near Charing Cross. She told me that she had been calling on several old friends, but had seen none of them,—some being really not at home, and others denying themselves to her. " I called," she said, " on Mrs. Siddons: I knew *she* was at home; yet I was not admitted." She was in such low spirits, that she even shed tears. I begged her to turn with me, and take a quiet dinner at St. James's Place; but she refused.

The " excellent writer," whom I quote in my Notes on *Human Life,* is Mrs. Inchbald. [" How often, says an excellent writer, do we err in our estimate of happiness! When I hear of a man who has noble parks, splendid palaces, and every luxury in life, I always inquire whom he has to love; and if I find he has nobody, or does not love those he has—in the midst of all his grandeur, I pronounce him a being in deep adversity."] The passage is from her *Nature and Art*.*

I have heard Crabbe describe his mingled feelings of hope and fear as he stood on London Bridge, when he first came up to town to try his fortune in the literary world.

The situation of domestic chaplain in a great family is generally a miserable one: what slights and mortifications attend it! Crabbe had had his share of such troubles in the Duke of Rutland's family; and I well remember that, at a London evening party, where the old Duchess of Rutland was present, he had a violent struggle with his feelings before he could prevail on himself to go up and pay his respects to her.

Crabbe, after his literary reputation had been established, was staying for a few days at the Old Hummums; but he was known to the

* But Mr. Rogers (as he frequently did when he quoted) has considerably altered the passage. Mrs. Inchbald's words are:—
" Some persons, I know, estimate happiness by fine houses, gardens, and parks,—others by pictures, horses, money, and various things wholly remote from their own species: but when I wish to ascertain the real felicity of any rational man, I always inquire *whom he has to love*. If I find he has nobody—or does not love those he has— even in the midst of all his profusion of finery and grandeur, I pronounce him a being in deep adversity." Vol. ii. 84, ed. 1796.

people in the coffee-room and to the waiters merely as "a Mr. Crabbe." One forenoon, when he had gone out, a gentleman called on him, and, while expressing his regret at not finding him at home, happened to let drop the information that "Mr. Crabbe was the celebrated poet." The next time that Crabbe entered the coffee-room, he was perfectly astonished at the sensation which he caused; the company were all eagerness to look at him, the waiters all officiousness to serve him.

Crabbe's early poetry is by far the best, as to *finish*. The conclusion of *The Library* is charmingly written;

" Go on, then, son of Vision! still pursue
    Thy airy dreams—the world is dreaming too.
    Ambition's lofty views, the pomp of state,
    The pride of wealth, the splendours of the
        great,
    Stripp'd of their mask, their cares and
        troubles known,
    Are visions far less happy than thy own:
    Go on! and, while the sons of care complain,
    Be wisely gay and innocently vain;
    While serious souls are by their fears undone,
    Blow sportive bladders in the beamy sun,
    And call them worlds! and bid the greatest
        show
    More radiant colours in their worlds below:
    Then, as they break, the slaves of care
        reprove,
    And tell them, Such are all the toys they love."

I asked him why he did not compose his later verses with equal care. He answered, "Because my reputation is already made." When he afterwards told me that he never produced more than *forty* verses a day, I said that he had better do as I do,—stint himself to *four*.

There is a familiarity in some parts of his *Tales* which makes one smile; yet it is by no means unpleasing; for example,—

" Letters were sent when franks could be
    procur'd,
  And when they could not, silence was
    endur'd."*

Crabbe used often to repeat with praise this couplet from Prior's *Solomon*,

" Abra was ready ere I call'd her name,
  And though I call'd another, Abra came."

It is some where cited by Sir Walter Scott;†
and I apprehend that Crabbe made it known
to him.

Other statesmen, besides Sir Robert Peel, have had very violent things said against them in the

* *The Frank Courtship*.
† Scott quotes it (not quite correctly) in *Rob Roy*.

House. Lord North once complained, in a speech, of " the brutal language " which Colonel Barrè had used towards him.—General Tarleton, not indeed in the House, but in private among his own party, said that " he was *glad to see* Fox's legs swelled."

Sir Robert Peel, in one of his communicative moods, told me that, when he was a boy, his father used to say to him, " Bob, you dog, if you are not prime minister some day, I'll disinherit you." I mentioned this to Sir Robert's sister, Mrs. Dawson, who assured me that she had often heard her father use those very words.

It is curious how fashion changes pronunciation. In my youth every body said " Lonnon," not " London ": Fox said " Lonnon " to the last; and so did Crowe. The now fashionable pronunciation of several words is to me at least very offensive: " cóntemplate " is bad enough; but " balcŏny " makes me sick.

When George Colman brought out his *Iron Chest*, he had not the civility to offer Godwin a box, or even to send him an order for admission, though the play was dramatised from *Caleb Williams*. Of this Godwin spoke with great bitterness.—Godwin was generally reckoned a disagreeable man; but I must say that *I* did not consider him such.*

Ah, the fate of my old acquaintance, Lady Salisbury! The very morning of the day on which the catastrophe occurred, I quitted Hatfield; and I then shook her by the hand,—that hand which was so soon to be a cinder. In the evening, after she had been dressed for dinner, her maid left her to go to tea. She was then writing letters; and it is supposed that, having stooped down her head,—for she was very short-sighted,—the flame of the candle caught her head-dress. Strange enough, but we had all remarked the day before, that Lady Salisbury seemed most unusually depressed in spirits!— Her eyes, as is generally the case with short-sighted persons, were so good, that she could read without spectacles: being very deaf, she would often read when in company; and, as she was a bad sleeper, she would sometimes read nearly the whole night.

Lady Salisbury never had any pretensions to beauty. In her youth she was dancing in a country-dance with the Prince of Wales at a ball given by the Duchess of Devonshire, when the

* One evening at Mr. Rogers's, when Godwin was present, the conversation turned on novels and romances. The company having agreed that *Don Quixote*, *Tom Jones*, and *Gil Blas*, were unrivalled in that species of composition, Mr. Rogers said, "Well, after these, *I* go to the sofa" (meaning, "*I* think that the next best are by Godwin," who happened to be sitting on the sofa). Quite unconscious of the compliment paid to him, Godwin exclaimed in great surprise, "What! do you admire *The Sofa?*" (a licentious novel by the younger Crebillon).

Prince suddenly quitted Lady Salisbury, and finished the dance with the Duchess. This rude behaviour of his Royal Highness drew forth some lines from Captain Morris.

[" Ungallant youth! could royal Edward see,
  While Salisbury's Garter decks thy faithless knee,
  That thou, false knight! hadst turn'd thy back, and fled
  From such a Salisbury as might wake the dead;
  Quick from thy treacherous breast her badge he'd tear,
  And strip the star that beauty planted there."]*

Madame de Staël one day said to me, " How sorry I am for Campbell! his poverty so unsettles his mind, that he cannot write." I replied, " Why does he not take the situation of a clerk? he could then compose verses during his leisure hours." This answer was reckoned very cruel both by Madame de Staël and Mackintosh: but there was really kindness as well as truth in it. When literature is the sole business of life,

---

* In her old age, Lady Salisbury met with another misfortune, at a ball at Hatfield House, when she was knocked over during a waltz. This incident produced the following impromptu by Joseph Jekyll:
  " Conservatives of Hatfield House
    Were surely harum-scarum;
    What could reforming Whigs do worse,
    Than knocking down old Sarum ? "
This was in 1834; and it is said that it is one of the first times the word *Conservative* was used, in place of the older *Tory.—Ed.*

it becomes a drudgery: when we are able to resort to it only at certain hours, it is a charming relaxation. In my earlier years I was a banker's clerk, obliged to be at the desk every day from ten till five o'clock; and I never shall forget the delight with which, on returning home, I used to read and write during the evening.

There are some of Campbell's lyrics which will never die. His *Pleasures of Hope* is no great favourite with me.* The *feeling* throughout his *Gertrude* is very beautiful; and one line, describing Gertrude's eyes, is exquisite,—" those eyes,"

" *That seem'd to love whate'er they look'd upon.*"

But that poem has passages which are monstrously incorrect: can any thing be worse in expression than—

* And it was much less so with Wordsworth, who criticised it to me nearly *verbatim* as follows; nor could his criticism, I apprehend, be easily refuted. " Campbell's *Pleasures of Hope* has been strangely overrated: its fine words and sounding lines please the generality of readers, who never stop to ask themselves the meaning of a passage. The lines,—

' Where Andes, giant of the western star,
  With meteor-standard to the winds unfurl'd,
  Looks from his throne of clouds o'er half the world,'

are sheer nonsense,—nothing more than a poetical indigestion. What has a giant to do with a star ? What is a meteor-standard ?— but it is useless to inquire what such stuff means. Once, at my house, Professor Wilson having spoken of those lines with great admiration, a very sensible and accomplished lady who happened to be present begged him to explain to her their meaning. He was extremely indignant; and, taking down the *Pleasures of Hope* from a shelf, read the lines aloud, and declared that they were splendid. ' Well, sir,' said the lady, ' *but what do they mean ?* ' Dashing the book on the floor, he exclaimed in his broad Scottish accent, ' I'll be daumed if I can tell!' "

" O Love! in such a wilderness as this,
   Where *transport and security entwine*,
   Here is *the empire of thy perfect bliss*,
   And here thou art indeed a god divine "?

I cannot forgive Goethe for certain things in his *Faust* and *Wilhelm Meister:* the man who appeals to the worst part of my nature commits a great offence.

The talking openly of their own merits is a " magnanimity " peculiar to foreigners. You remember the angry surprise which Lamartine expresses at Lady Hester Stanhope's never having heard of him,—of him, a person so celebrated over all the world!

Lamartine is a man of genius, but very affected. Talleyrand (when in London) invited me to meet him, and placed me beside him at dinner. I asked him, " Are you acquainted with Beranger? " " No; he wished to be introduced to me, but I declined it."—" I would go," said I, " a league to see him." This was nearly all our conversation: he did not choose to talk. In short, he was so disagreeable, that, some days after, both Talleyrand and the Duchess di Dino apologised to me for his ill-breeding.

At present new plays seem hardly to be

regarded as literature; people may go to see them acted, but no one thinks of reading them. During the run of *Paul Pry*, I happened to be at a dinner-party where every body was talking about it,—that is, about Liston's performance of the hero. I asked first one person, then another, and then another, who was the author of it? Not a man or woman in the company knew that it was written by Poole!

When people have had misunderstandings with each other, and are anxious to be again on good terms, they ought never to make attempts at reconciliation by means of letters; *they should see each other*. Sir Walter Scott quarrelled with Lady Roslin, in consequence, I believe, of some expressions he had used about Fox. "If Scott," said she, "instead of writing to me on the subject, had *only* paid me a visit, I must have forgiven him."

There had been for some time a coolness between Lord Durham and myself; and I was not a little annoyed to find that I was to sit next him at one of the Royal Academy dinners: I requested the stewards to change my place at the table; but it was too late to make any alteration. We sat down. Lord Durham took no notice of me. At last I said to him, "Will your lordship do me the honour of drinking a glass of wine with me?" He answered, "Certainly, on condition that you will come and dine with me soon."

This is not a bad charade: What is it that causes a cold, cures a cold, and pays the doctor? A draft.

I hope to read Ariosto through once more before I die, if not in the original, in Harington's translation, which in some parts is very well done; in one part,—the story of Jocondo,—admirably.

Rose's* version is so bald, that it wearies me. I read the whole of it, by Rose's desire, in the proof sheets.—At one time Rose gave himself up so entirely to Italian, that he declared " he felt some difficulty in using his native language."

Once, when Rose complained to me of being unhappy " from the recollection of having done many things which he wished he had not done," I comforted him by replying, " I know that during your life you have done many kind and generous things; but *them* you have forgotten, because *a man's good deeds fade away from his memory, while those which are the reverse keep constantly recurring to it.*"

He was in a sad state of mental imbecility shortly before his death. When people attempted to enter into conversation with him, he would continue to ask them two questions,— " When did Sir Walter Scott die? " and " How is Lord Holland? " (who was already dead.) But I, aware that no subject is so exciting to an author as that of his own writings, spoke to

* William Stewart Rose (1775–1843).—*Ed.*

Rose about his various publications; and, for a while, he talked of them rationally enough.

Lord Grenville has more than once said to me at Dropmore, " What a frightful mistake it was to send such a person as Lord Castlereagh to the Congress of Vienna! a man who was so ignorant, that he did not know the map of Europe; and who could be won over to make any concessions by only being asked to breakfast with the Emperor."

Castlereagh's education had been sadly neglected; but he possessed considerable talents, and was very amiable.

I have read Gilpin's *Life of Cranmer* several times through. What an interesting account he gives of the manner in which Cranmer passed the day!—I often repeat a part of Cranmer's prayer at the stake,—" O blessed Redeemer, who assumed not a mortal shape *for small offences, who died not to atone for venial sins,*" &c.

I don't call *Robinson Crusoe* and *Gulliver's Travels* " novels: " they stand quite unrivalled for invention among all prose fictions.

When I was at Banbury, I happened to observe in the churchyard several inscriptions to the memory of persons named Gulliver; and, on my return home, looking into *Gulliver's Travels*, I found, to my surprise, that the said inscriptions are mentioned there as a confirmation of Mr. Gulliver's statement that "his family came from Oxfordshire."

I am not sure that I would not rather have written Manzoni's *Promessi Sposi* than all Scott's novels. Manzoni's mother was a daughter of the famous Beccaria; and I remember seeing her about sixty years ago at the house of the father of the Misses Berry: she was a very lively agreeable woman.

Bowles, like most other poets, was greatly depressed by the harsh criticisms of the reviewers. I advised him not to mind them; and, eventually following my advice, he became a much happier man. I suggested to him the subject of *The Missionary;* and he was to dedicate it to me. He, however, dedicated it to a noble lord, who never, either by word or letter, acknowledged the dedication.

Bowles's nervous timidity is* the most ridiculous

* Wordsworth, Mrs. Wordsworth, their daughter, and Bowles, went upon the Thames in a boat, one fine summer's day. Though the water was smooth as glass, Bowles very soon became so alarmed, that he insisted on being set ashore; upon which Wordsworth said to him, "Your confessing your cowardice is the most striking instance of valour that I ever met with." This was told to me by Wordsworth himself.—What follows is from my Memoranda of Wordsworth's conversation. "When Bowles's Sonnets first appeared,—a thin 4to pamphlet, entitled *Fourteen Sonnets,*—I bought them in a walk through London with my dear brother, who was afterwards drowned at sea. I read them as we went along; and to the great annoyance of my brother, I stopped in a niche of London Bridge to finish the pamphlet. Bowles's short pieces are his best: his long poems are rather *flaccid*."

thing imaginable. Being passionately fond of music, he came to London expressly to attend the last Commemoration of Handel. After going into the Abbey, he observed that the door was closed: immediately he ran to the doorkeeper, exclaiming, " What! am I to be *shut up* here? " and out he went, before he had heard a single note. I once bought a stall-ticket for him, that he might accompany me to the Opera; but, just as we were stepping into the carriage, he said, " Dear me, your horses seem uncommonly frisky "; and he stayed at home.

" I never," said he, " had but one watch; and I lost it the very first day I wore it." Mrs. Bowles whispered to me, " And if he got another to-day, he would lose it as quickly."

Major Price* was a great favourite with George the Third, and ventured to say any thing to him. They were walking together in the grounds at Windsor Castle, when the following dialogue took place. " I shall certainly," said the King, " order this tree to be cut down." " If it is cut down, your majesty will have destroyed the finest tree about the Castle."—" People are always contradicting me: I will not be contradicted." " Permit me to observe, that if your majesty will not allow people to speak, you will never hear the truth."—" Well, Price, I believe you are right."

* Brother to Sir Uvedale Price, and for many years vice-chamberlain to Queen Charlotte.

When the Duke of Clarence (William the Fourth) was a very young man, he happened to be dining at the Equerries' table. Among the company was Major Price. The Duke told one of his facetious stories. " Excellent! " said Price; " I wish I could believe it."—" If you say that again, Price," cried the Duke, " I'll send this claret at your head." Price *did* say it again. Accordingly the claret *came*,—and it was *returned*. —I had this from Lord St. Helens, who was one of the party.

Once, when in company with William the Fourth, I quite forgot that it is against all etiquette to ask a sovereign about his health; and, on his saying to me, " Mr. Rogers, I hope you are well," I replied, " Very well, I thank your majesty: *I trust that your majesty is quite well also*." Never was a king in greater confusion; he didn't know where to look, and stammered out, " Yes,—yes,—only a little rheumatism."

I have several times breakfasted with the Princesses at Buckingham House. The Queen (Charlotte) always breakfasted with the King: but she would join us afterwards, and read the newspapers to us, or converse very agreeably.

Dining one day with the Princess of Wales (Queen Caroline), I heard her say that on her first arrival in this country, she could speak only *one* word of English. Soon after, I mentioned that circumstance to a large party; and a discussion arose what English word would be most useful for a person to know, supposing that person's knowledge of the language must be limited to a single word. The greater number of the company fixed on " Yes." But Lady Charlotte Lindsay said that she should prefer " No "; because, though " Yes " never meant " No,"—" No " very often meant " Yes."

The Princess was very good-natured and agreeable. She once sent to me at four o'clock in the afternoon, to say that she was coming to sup with me that night. I returned word, that I should feel highly honoured by her coming, but that unfortunately it was too late to make up a party to meet her. She came, however, bringing with her Sir William Drummond.

One night, after dining with her at Kensington Palace, I was sitting in the carriage, waiting for Sir Henry Englefield to accompany me to town, when a sentinel, at about twenty yards' distance from me, was struck dead by a flash of lightning. I never beheld any thing like that flash: it was a body of flame, in the centre of which were quivering zigzag fires, such as artists put into the hand of Jupiter; and, after being visible for a moment, it seemed to explode. I immediately returned to the hall of the Palace, where I found the servants standing in terror, with their faces against the wall.

I was to dine on a certain day with the Princess of Wales at Kensington, and, thinking that Ward (Lord Dudley) was to be of the party, I wrote to him, proposing that we should go together. His answer was, " Dear Rogers,

I am not invited. The fact is, when I dined there last, I made several rather free jokes; and the Princess, taking me perhaps for a clergyman, has not asked me back again."

One night, at Kensington, I had the Princess for my partner in a country-dance of fourteen couple. I exerted myself to the utmost; but not quite to her satisfaction, for she kept calling out to me, " Vite, vite! "

She was fond of going to public places incog. One forenoon, she sent me a note to say that she wished me to accompany her that evening to the theatre; but I had an engagement which I did not choose to give up, and declined accompanying her. She took offence at this; and our intercourse was broken off till we met in Italy. I was at an inn about a stage from Milan, when I saw Queen Caroline's carriages in the court-yard. I kept myself quite close, and drew down the blinds of the sitting room: but the good-natured Queen found out that I was there, and, coming to my window, knocked on it with her knuckles. In a moment we were the best friends possible; and there, as afterwards in other parts of Italy, I dined and spent the day with her. Indeed, I once travelled during a whole night in the same carriage with her and Lady Charlotte Campbell; when the shortness of her majesty's legs not allowing her to rest them on the seat opposite, she wheeled herself round, and very coolly placed them on the lap of Lady Charlotte, who was sitting next to her.

I remember Brighton before the Pavilion was built; and in those days I have seen the Prince of Wales drinking tea in a public room of what was then the chief inn, just as other people did.

At a great party given by Henry Hope in Cavendish Square, Lady Jersey* said she had something particular to tell me; so, not to be interrupted, we went into the gallery. As we were walking along it, we met the Prince of Wales, who, on seeing Lady Jersey, stopped for a moment, and then, drawing himself up, marched past her with a look of the utmost disdain. Lady Jersey returned the look to the full; and, as soon as the Prince was gone, said to me with a smile, " Didn't I do it well? "—I was taking a drive with Lady Jersey in her carriage, when I expressed (with great sincerity) my regret at being unmarried, saying that " if I had a wife, I should have somebody *to care about me*." " Pray, Mr. Rogers," said Lady J., " how could you be sure that your wife would not *care more about somebody else than about you?* "

* " The Prince one day said to Colonel Willis, ' I am determined to break off my intimacy with Lady Jersey; and you must deliver the letter which announces to her my determination.' When Willis put it into Lady Jersey's hand, she said, before opening it, ' You have brought me a gilded dagger.'—Willis was on such familiar terms with the Prince, that he ventured to give his advice about his conduct. ' If your royal highess,' he said, ' would only show yourself at the theatre or in the park, in company with the Princess, two or three times a year, the public would be quite content, and would not trouble themselves about your domestic proceedings.' The Prince replied, ' Really, Willis, with the exception of Lord Moira, nobody ever presumed to speak to me as you do.' The Prince was anxious to get rid of Lord Moira; and hence his lordship's splendid banishment.—These anecdotes were told to me by Willis."—*Maltby*.

I was staying at Lord Bathurst's, when he had to communicate to the Prince Regent the death of the Princess Charlotte. The circumstances were these. Lord Bathurst was suddenly roused in the middle of the night by the arrival of a messenger to inform him that the Princess was dead. After a short consultation with his family, Lord Bathurst went to the Duke of York; and his royal highness having immediately dressed himself, they proceeded together to Carlton House. On reaching it, they asked to see Sir Benjamin Bloomfield; and telling him what had occurred, they begged him to convey the melancholy tidings to the Prince Regent. He firmly refused to do so. They then begged Sir Benjamin to inform the Prince that they requested to see him on a matter of great importance. A message was brought back by Sir Benjamin, that the Prince already knew all they had to tell him, —viz. that the Princess had been delivered, and that the child was dead,—and that he declined seeing them at present. They again, by means of Sir Benjamin, urged their request; and were at last admitted into the Prince's chamber. He was sitting up in bed; and, as soon as they entered, he repeated what he had previously said by message,—that he already knew all they had to tell him, &c. Lord Bathurst then communicated the fatal result of the Princess's confinement. On hearing it, the Prince Regent struck his forehead violently with both his hands, and fell forward into the arms of the Duke of York. Among other exclamations which this intelligence drew from him, was, " Oh, what will become of that poor man (Prince Leopold)! " —Yet, only six or seven hours had elapsed when he was busily arranging all the pageantry for his daughter's funeral.

The Duchess of Buckingham told me that, when George the Fourth slept at Stowe in the state bedchamber (which has a good deal of ebony furniture), it was lighted up with a vast number of wax candles, which were kept burning the whole night.—Nobody, I imagine, except a king, has any liking for a state bedchamber. I was at Cassiobury with a large party, when a gentleman arrived, to whom Lord Essex said, " I must put you into the state bedroom, as it is the only one unoccupied." The gentleman, rather than sleep in it, took up his quarters at the inn.

No one had more influence over George the Fourth than Sir William Knighton. Lawrence (the painter) told me that he was once dining at the palace when the King said to Knighton that he was resolved to discharge a partic- ular attendant immediately. " Sir," replied Knighton, " he is an excellent servant."—" I am determined to discharge him," said the King. " Sir," replied Knighton, " he is an excellent servant."—" Well, well," said the King, " let him remain till I think further of it."— Speaking of Knighton to an intimate friend, George the Fourth remarked, " My obligations to Sir William Knighton are greater than to any man alive: he has arranged all my accounts, and brought perfect order out of chaos."

One day when George the Fourth was talking about his youthful exploits, he mentioned, with particular satisfaction, that he had made a body of troops charge down the Devil's Dyke (near Brighton). Upon which the Duke of Wellington merely observed to him, " Very steep, sir."

I was told by the Duchess-Countess of Sutherland what Sir Henry Halford had told her,— that, when George the Fourth was very near his end, he said to him, " Pray, Sir Henry, keep these women from me " (alluding to certain ladies).

I'll tell you an anecdote of Napoleon, which I had from Talleyrand. " Napoleon," said T., " was at Boulogne with the Army of England, when he received intelligence that the Austrians, under Mack, were at Ulm. ' If it had been mine to place them,' exclaimed Napoleon, ' I should have placed them there.' In a moment the army was on the march, and he at Paris. I attended him to Strasburg. We were there at the house of the Prefet, and no one in the room but ourselves, when Napoleon was suddenly seized with a fit, foaming at the mouth: he cried ' Fermez la porte! ' and then lay senseless on the floor. I bolted the door. Presently, Berthier knocked. ' On ne peut pas entrer.' Afterwards, Josephine knocked; to whom I addressed the same words. Now, what a situation would mine have been, if Napoleon had died! But he recovered in about half an hour.

Next morning, by daybreak, he was in his carriage; and within sixty hours the Austrian army had capitulated."

I repeated the anecdote to Lucien Buonaparte,* who listened with great sang froid. " Did you ever hear this before? " " Never: but many great men have been subject to fits; for instance, Julius Cæsar. My brother on another occasion had an attack of the same kind; but that " (and he smiled) " was after being defeated."†

On my asking Talleyrand if Napoleon was really married to Josephine, he replied, " Pas tout-à-fait."

I asked him which was the best portrait of Napoleon. He said, " That which represents him at Malmaison: it is by Isabey. The marble bust of Napoleon by Canova, which I gave to A. Baring, is an excellent likeness."

" Did Napoleon shave himself? " I inquired. " Yes," answered Talleyrand, " but very slowly, and conversing during the operation. He used to say that kings by birth were shaved by others, but that he who has made himself *Roi* shaves himself."

To my question—whether the despatch which Napoleon published on his retreat from Moscow was written by Napoleon himself,—Talleyrand replied, " By himself, certainly."

* Mr. Rogers was very intimate with Lucien, and liked him much; yet he could not resist occasionally laughing at some things in his *Charlemagne;* for instance, at,—

" L'ange maudit admire et contemple Judas."

† An allusion to an adventure with an actress.

222

Dr. Lawrence assured me that Burke shortened his life by the frequent use of emetics,— "he was always tickling his throat with a feather." He complained of an oppression at his chest, which he fancied emetics would remove.

Malone (than whom no one was more intimate with Burke) persisted to the last in saying that, if *Junius's Letters* were not written by Burke, they were at least written by some person who had received great assistance from Burke in composing them; and he was strongly inclined to fix the authorship of them upon Dyer.* Burke had a great friendship for Dyer, whom he considered to be a man of transcendent abilities; and it was reported, that, upon Dyer's death, Burke secured and suppressed all the papers which he had left behind him.

I once dined at Dilly's in company with Woodfall, who then declared in the most positive terms that *he* did not know who Junius was.

A story appeared in the newspapers, that an unknown individual had died at Marlborough, and that, in consequence of his desire expressed just before his death, the word *Junius* had been placed over his grave. Now, Sir James Mackintosh and I, happening to be at Marlborough, resolved to inquire into the truth of this story. We accordingly went into the shop of a bookseller, a respectable-looking old man with a velvet cap, and asked him what he knew about it.

* Samuel Dyer.

223

" I have *heard*," said he, " that a person was buried here with that inscription on his grave; but I have not *seen* it." He then called out to his daughter, " What do you know about it, Nan? " " I have *heard*," replied Nan, " that there is such a grave; but I have not *seen* it." We next applied to the sexton; and his answer was, " I have *heard* of such a grave; but I have not *seen* it." Nor did we *see* it, you may be sure, though we took the trouble of going into the churchyard.*

My own impression is, that the *Letters of Junius* were written by Sir Philip Francis. In a speech, which I once heard him deliver, at the Mansion House, concerning the Partition of Poland, I had a striking proof that Francis possessed no ordinary powers of eloquence.

I was one day conversing with Lady Holland in her dressing-room, when Sir Philip Francis was announced. " Now," she said, " I *will* ask him if he is Junius." I was about to withdraw; but she insisted on my staying. Sir Philip entered, and, soon after he was seated, she put the question to him. His answer was, " Madam, do you mean to insult me? "—and he went on to say, that when he was a younger man,

* A friend observed to me,—" Mr. Rogers and Sir James should have gone, not to Marlborough, but to Hungerford; and there they would have found a tomb with this inscription, *Stat nominis umbra;* which is the motto of Junius; and hence the tomb is called *Junius's tomb*." I mentioned this to Mr. Rogers, who said, " It may be so; but what I told you about our inquiries at Marlborough is fact; and a good story it is."

people would not have ventured to charge him with being the author of those Letters.*

When Lady Holland wanted to get rid of a fop she used to say, " I beg your pardon,—but I wish you would sit a little further off; there is something on your handkerchief which I don't quite like."

When any gentleman, to her great annoyance, was standing with his back close to the chimney-piece, she would call out, " Have the goodness, sir, to stir the fire! "

Her delight was to conquer all difficulties that might oppose her will. Near Tunbridge there is (at least, there was) a house which no stranger was allowed to see. Lady Holland never ceased till she got permission to inspect it; and through it she marched in triumph, taking a train of people with her, even her maid.

When she and Lord Holland were at Naples, Murat and his Queen used to have certain evenings appointed for receiving persons of distinction. Lady Holland would not go to those royal parties. At last Murat, who was always anxious to conciliate the English government, gave a concert expressly in honour of Lady Holland; and she had the gratification of sitting, at that concert, between Murat and the Queen,

---

* The following notice must be referred, I presume, to an earlier occasion. " Brougham was by when Francis made the often-quoted answer to Rogers—' There is a question, Sir Philip (said R.), which I should much like to ask, if you will allow me.' ' You had better not, sir (answered Francis); you may have reason to be sorry for it (or repent of it).' The addition [by the newspapers] to this story is, that Rogers, on leaving him, muttered to himself, ' If he *is* Junius, it must be *Junius Brutus*.' "—Moore's *Memoirs*, &c., vol. vi. 66.

when, no doubt, she applied to them her screw,—
that is, she fairly asked them about every thing
which she wished to know.—By the by, Murat
and his Queen were extremely civil to me. The
Queen once talked to me about *The Pleasures of
Memory*. I often met Murat when he was on
horseback, and he would invariably call out to
me, rising in his stirrups, " Hé bien, monsieur,
êtes-vous inspiré aujourdhui? "

Lord Holland never ventured to ask any one
to dinner (not even me, whom he had known
so long and so intimately) without previously
consulting Lady H. Shortly before his death,
I called at Holland House, and found only Lady
H. within. As I was coming out, I met Lord
Holland, who said, " Well, do you return to
dinner? " I answered, " No; I have not been
invited."—Perhaps this deference to Lady H.*
was not to be regretted; for Lord Holland was
so hospitable and good-natured, that, had he
been left to himself, he would have had a crowd
at his table daily.

What a disgusting thing is the *fagging* at our
great schools! When Lord Holland was a
schoolboy, he was forced, as a fag, to toast
bread *with his fingers* for the breakfast of another
boy. Lord H.'s mother sent him a toasting-
fork. His fagger broke it over his head, and

* Lady Holland was not among Mr. Rogers's earliest acquaintances
in the great world.—Mr. Richard Sharp once said to him, " When
do you mean to give up the society of Lady Jersey? " Mr. Rogers
replied, " When you give up that of Lady Holland,"—little thinking
then that she was eventually to be one of his own most intimate
friends.

still compelled him to prepare the toast in the old way. In consequence of this process his fingers suffered so much that they always retained a withered appearance.

Lord Holland persisted in saying that pictures gave him more pain than pleasure. He also hated music; yet, in some respects, he had a very good ear, for he was a capital mimic.

What a pity it is that Luttrell* gives up nearly his whole time to persons of mere fashion! Every thing that he has written is very clever.

None of the *talkers* whom I meet in London society can slide in a brilliant thing with such readiness as he does.

I was one day not a little surprised at being told by Moore that, in consequence of the article on his *Poems* in *The Edinburgh Review*, he had called out Jeffrey, who at that time was in London. He asked me to lend him a pair of pistols: I said, and truly, that I had none.†
Moore then went to William Spencer to borrow pistols, and to talk to him about the duel; and Spencer, who was delighted with this confidence, did not fail to blab the matter to Lord Fincastle,

* Henry Luttrell (1765 ?–1851), wit and conversationalist.—*Ed.*

† " William Spencer being *the only one of all my friends* whom I thought likely to furnish me with these *sine-qua-nons* [pistols], I hastened to confide to him my wants," &c.   Moore's *Memoirs*, &c. vol. i. 222.   But Moore's recollection of the particulars connected with the duel was somewhat imperfect: see the next note.

and also, I believe, to some women of rank.—I was at Spencer's house in the forenoon, anxious to learn the issue of the duel, when a messenger arrived with the tidings that Moore and Jeffrey were in custody, and with a request from Moore that Spencer would bail him. Spencer did not seem much inclined to do so, remarking that " he could not well go out, for it was *already twelve o'clock*, and he had to be dressed *by four!* " So I went to Bow Street and bailed Moore.*— The question now was, whether Moore and Jeffrey should still fight or not. I secretly consulted General Fitzpatrick, who gave it as his decided opinion that " Mr. Jeffrey was not called upon to accept a second challenge," insinuating, of course, that Moore was bound to send one. I took care not to divulge what the General had said: and the poet and critic were eventually reconciled by means of Horner and myself: they shook hands with each other in the garden behind my house.

So heartily has Moore repented of having published *Little's Poems*,† that I have seen him shed tears,—tears of deep contrition,—when we were talking of them.

Young ladies read his *Lalla Rookh* without

* " Though I had sent for William Spencer, I am not quite sure that it was he that acted as my bail, or whether it was not Rogers that so officiated. I am, however, certain that the latter joined us at the office," &c. Moore's *Memoirs*, &c. vol. i. 205.

† Moore's early poems were published under this designation. Hence Byron:
> " 'Tis Little, young Catullus of his day,
> As sweet, but as immoral, in his lay."
> —*Ed.*

being aware (I presume) of the grossness of
The Veiled Prophet. These lines by Mr. Sneyd
are amusing enough;

> " *Lalla Rookh*
> Is a naughty book
> By Tommy Moore,
> Who has written four,
> Each warmer
> Than the former,
> So the most recent
> Is the least decent."

Moore borrowed from me Lord Thurlow's
Poems, and forthwith wrote that ill-natured
article on them in *The Edinburgh Review*. It
made me angry; for Lord Thurlow, with all his
eccentricity, was a man of genius: but the public
chose to laugh at him, and Moore, who always
follows the world's opinion, of course did so too.
—I like Thurlow's verses on Sidney.*

Moore once said to me, " I am much fonder
of reading works in prose than in verse." I
replied, " I should have known so from your
writings "; and I meant the words as a compliment:—his best poems are quite original.

Moore is a very worthy man, but not a little
improvident. His excellent wife contrives to
maintain the whole family on a guinea a-week;
and he, when in London, thinks nothing of
throwing away that sum weekly on hackney-

---

* Let me add, that Lord Thurlow's sonnet *To a bird that haunted
the waters of Laken in the winter* was a favourite with Charles Lamb.

coaches and gloves. I said to him, " You must have made ten thousand pounds by your musical publications." He replied, " More than that." In short, he has received for his various works nearly thirty thousand pounds. When, owing to the state of his affairs, he found it necessary to *retire* for a while, I advised him to make Holyrood House his refuge: there he could have lived cheaply and comfortably, with permission to walk about unmolested every Sunday, when he might have dined with Walter Scott or Jeffrey. But he *would* go to Paris; and there he spent about a thousand a-year.

At the time when Moore was struggling with his grief for the loss of his children, he said to me, " What a wonderful man that Shakespeare is! how perfectly I now feel the truth of his words,—

" And if I laugh at any mortal thing,
   'Tis that I may not weep "!

I happened to repeat to Mrs. N. what Moore had said; upon which she observed, " Why, the passage is not Shakespeare's, but Byron's." And sure enough we found it in *Don Juan.**

* C. iv. 4. (Moore had forgotten that he had quoted the passage as Byron's in his *Life of Byron*).—Richardson had said the same thing long ago:—" Indeed, it is to this deep concern that my levity is owing: for I struggle and struggle, and try to buffet down my cruel reflections as they rise; and when I cannot, *I am forced*, as I have often said, *to try to make myself laugh, that I may not cry;* for one or other I must do: and is it not philosophy carried to the highest pitch, for a man to conquer such tumults of soul as I am sometimes agitated by, and, in the very height of the storm, to be able to quaver out an horse-laugh ? " *Clarissa Harlowe*, Letter 84, vol. vii. 319.

Another lady, who was present, having declared that she did not understand it, I said, " I will give you an illustration of it. A friend of mine was chiding his daughter. She laughed. ' Now,' continued the father, ' you make matters worse by laughing.' She then burst into tears, exclaiming, ' If I do not laugh, I must cry.' "

Moore has now taken to an amusement which is very well suited to the fifth act of life;—he plays cribbage every night with Mrs. Moore.

In the *Memoir* of Cary by his son, Coleridge is said to have first become acquainted with Cary's *Dante* when he met the translator at Little Hampton. But that is a mistake.* Moore mentioned the work to me with great admiration; I mentioned it to Wordsworth;† and he to Coleridge, who had never heard of it till then, and who forthwith read it.

I was present at that lecture by Coleridge, during which he spoke of Cary's *Dante* in high terms of praise: there were about a hundred and twenty persons in the room. But I doubt if that did much towards making it known. It owes some of its celebrity to me; for the article on Dante in *The Edinburgh Review*, which

* I think the mistake was Rogers's. Dykes Campbell in his *Samuel Taylor Coleridge* (p. 232) places the meeting in September, 1817. The story is that Cary was reciting Homer on the beach to his son, and that thereupon Coleridge, very naturally, introduced himself.—*Ed.*

† Wordsworth once remarked to me, " It is a disgrace to the age that Cary has no church-preferment; I think his translation of Dante a great national work."

was written by Foscolo, has very considerable additions by Mackintosh, and a few by myself. Cary was aware (though his biographer evidently is not) that I had written a portion of that article; yet he never mentioned it to me: perhaps there was something in it which he did not like.

On the resignation of Baber, chief librarian at the British Museum, I wrote a letter to the Archbishop of Canterbury, urging Cary's claim to fill the vacant place.* The Archbishop replied, that his only reason for not giving Cary his vote was the unfortunate circumstance of Cary's having been more than once, in consequence of domestic calamities, afflicted with temporary alienation of mind.† I had quite forgotten this; and I immediately wrote again to the Archbishop, saying that I now agreed with him concerning Cary's unfitness for the situation. I also, as delicately as I could, touched on the subject to Cary himself, telling him that the place was not suited for him.

After another gentleman‡ had been appointed Baber's successor, the trustees of the Museum recommended Cary to the Government for a pension,—which they seemed resolved not to grant; and I made more than one earnest application to them in his behalf. At last Lord Melbourne sent Lord E. to me with a message

* Cary, as assistant-librarian, stood next in succession.

† It appears, however, from the *Memoir of Cary* by his son (vol. ii. 285), that afterwards, the Archbishop, in consequence of a medical certificate of Cary's fitness for the office, was desirous that he should be appointed, " but could not prevail on his co-trustees to concur with him."

‡ Antonio Panizzi.—*Ed.*

that " there was very little money to dispose of, but that Cary should have 100*l.* per annum." I replied that " it was so small a sum, that I did not choose to mention the offer to Cary; and that, as soon as Sir Robert Peel came into office, I should apply to him for a larger sum, with confident hopes of better success." Lord Melbourne then let me know that Cary should have 200*l.* a-year; which I accepted for him.

Cary never forgave me for my conduct in the Museum business; and never afterwards called upon me. But I met him one day in the Park, when he said (much to his credit, considering his decided political opinions) that " he was better pleased to receive 200*l.* a-year from Lord Melbourne than double the sum from Sir Robert Peel."

Visiting Lady —— one day, I made inquiries about her sister. " She is now staying with me," answered Lady ——, " but she is unwell in consequence of a fright which she got on her way from Richmond to London." At that time omnibuses were great rarities; and while Miss —— was coming to town, the footman, observing an omnibus approach, and thinking that she might like to see it, suddenly called in at the carriage-window, " Ma'am, the omnibus! " Miss ——, being unacquainted with the term, and not sure but an *omnibus* might be a wild beast escaped from the Zoological Gardens, was thrown into a dreadful state of agitation by the announcement.

I think Sheridan Knowles by far the best writer of plays since those whom we call *our old dramatists.*—Macready's performance of Tell (in Knowles's *William Tell*) is first-rate. No actor ever affected me more than Macready did in some scenes of that play.

Words cannot do justice to Theodore Hook's talent for improvisation: it was perfectly wonderful. He was one day sitting at the pianoforte, singing an extempore song as fluently as if he had had the words and music before him, when Moore happened to look into the room, and Hook instantly introduced a long parenthesis,

" And here's Mr. Moore,
Peeping in at the door," &c.—

The last time I saw Hook was in the lobby of Lord Canterbury's house after a large evening party there. He was walking up and down, singing with great gravity, to the astonishment of the footmen, " Shepherds, I have lost my *hat.*"

When Erskine was made Lord Chancellor, Lady Holland never rested till she prevailed on

him to give Sidney Smith a living.* Smith
went to thank him for the appointment. " Oh,"
said Erskine, " don't thank *me*, Mr. Smith. I
gave you the living because Lady Holland
insisted on my doing so: and if she had
desired me to give it to the devil, *he* must have
had it."

At one time, when I gave a dinner, I used to
have candles placed all round the dining-room,
and high up, in order to show off the pictures.
I asked Smith how he liked that plan. " Not
at all," he replied; " above, there is a blaze of
light, and below, nothing but darkness and
gnashing of teeth."

He said that —— was so fond of contradiction,
that he would throw up the window in the middle
of the night, and contradict the watchman who
was calling the hour.

When his physician advised him to " take a
walk upon an empty stomach," Smith asked,
" Upon whose? "

" Lady Cork," said Smith, " was once so
moved by a charity sermon, that she begged me
to lend her a guinea for her contribution. I did
so. She never repaid me, and spent it on
herself."

He said that " *his* idea of heaven was eating
fois gras to the sound of trumpets."

" I had a very odd dream last night," said he;
" I dreamed that there were thirty-nine Muses
and nine Articles: and my head is still quite
confused about them."

* The living of Foston-le-Clay in Yorkshire.

Smith said, " The Bishop of —— is so like Judas, that I now firmly believe in the Apostolical Succession."

Witty as Smith was, I have seen him at my own house absolutely overpowered by the superior facetiousness of William Bankes.

Speaking to me of Buonaparte, the Duke of Wellington remarked, that in one respect he was superior to all the generals who had ever existed. " Was it," I asked, " in the management and skilful arrangement of his troops? "—" No," answered the Duke; " it was in his power of concentrating such vast masses of men,—a most important point in the art of war."

" I have found," said the Duke, " that raw troops, however inferior to the old ones in manœuvring, are far superior to them in downright hard fighting with the enemy: at Waterloo, the young ensigns and lieutenants, who had never before seen a battle, rushed to meet death as if they had been playing at cricket."

The Duke thinks very highly of Napier's *History:* its only fault, he says, is—that Napier is sometimes apt to convince himself that a thing must be true, because *he* wishes to believe it.—Of Southey's *History* he merely said, " I don't think much of *it.*"

Of the Duke's perfect coolness on the most trying occasions, Colonel Gurwood gave me this instance. He was once in great danger of being drowned at sea. It was bed-time, when the captain of the vessel came to him, and said, " It will soon be all over with us."—" Very well," answered the Duke, " then I shall not take off my boots."

The Duke says that the Lord's Prayer alone is an evidence of the truth of Christianity,—so admirably is that prayer accommodated to all our wants.—I took the Sacrament with the Duke at Strathfieldsaye; and nothing could be more striking than his unaffected devotion.

When I was at Paris, I went to Alexis,* and desired him to describe to me my house in St. James's Place.   On my word, he astonished me! He described most exactly the peculiarities of the staircase,—said that not far from the window in the drawing-room there was a picture of a man in armour (the painting by Giorgione), &c. &c.

Colonel Gurwood, shortly before his death, assured me that he was reminded by Alexis of some circumstances which had happened to him in Spain, and which he could not conceive how any human being, except himself, should know.

Still, I cannot believe in clairvoyance,— *because the thing is impossible.*

* The celebrated clairvoyant.

APPENDIX

In the Dyce Collection at the library of the Victoria & Albert Museum, and in the Forster Collection at the same place, are two interesting items which throw a little additional light on the *Recollections of the Table-talk of Samuel Rogers.* The first (D. 3403) is Dyce's own copy of the third edition of the book with a few manuscript notes in what appears to be his own hand. The other (F. 2656) is a bound volume of the proof-sheets for the book, with numerous corrections.

In the latter are a number of anecdotes that Dyce evidently decided to reject. A few of them are, I think, worth preserving, though with the proviso that he may well have omitted them because, on second thoughts, he doubted their authenticity.

The first of these, which comes between the second and third paragraphs on page 147 of the present edition, concerns Coleridge, and is as follows: " At a dinner-party, among other abuse which he poured out on the Unitarians, he declared that ' they were fools.' Lord Holland, who was present, observed, ' Then the Trinitarians must be three fools.' "

Page 192 of present edition, between paragraphs two and three: " As Moore resided chiefly in Wiltshire, he saw comparatively little of Byron. After I had become intimate with Byron,—and our acquaintance with each other was quickly followed by intimacy,—I saw him regularly every day, nearly up to the time of his marriage, when I went to Italy, and did not return to England till shortly before his separation from Lady Byron." [In fact, Rogers did not go to Italy until some nine months after Byron's marriage, and had been back in England almost as long before the separation.]

Page 192, the passage dealing with the burning of Byron's *Memoirs* and now reading, " Moore, I conceive, was not justified in giving his consent to the burning," originally read: " Moore had no right to burn Byron's [Memoirs], which were given, not to him, but to his son."

Page 197, between paragraphs one and two: " Writing a note to Byron at Venice, I quoted in it my own (then unpublished) lines,—' There is a glorious city in the sea,' etc., without letting him know they were mine. On our next meeting, he showed that he liked them by repeating them to me. He thought that they were by Southey, whose poetry he admired, though he wished the world to believe that he despised it.

In another note (at Venice) I asked him ' if he had *wedded the Adriatic?* ' He replied, ' No: but if the Doge will marry my wife, I'll wed the Adriatic to-morrow.' "

Page 207, between paragraphs two and three: " When Lord Charlemont (then a young man) was travelling through France with another Englishman, they called upon Montesquieu, who received them very kindly. He took them into his garden; and coming to a gate which was locked, he leaped over it as nimbly as if he had been only twenty.—There was great simplicity of character in Montesquieu. During his visit to England somebody played him the trick which is played on Parson Adams in Fielding's *Joseph Andrews*—making him tumble into a tub full of water, which, having a cloth over it, looked like a seat."

Page 218, footnote: after " his lordship's splendid banishment", the passage originally read: " The Prince was at Liverpool, with Roscoe, when the news of Fox's death first reached him; the instant he heard it, he burst into tears, exclaiming, ' Fox was the truest friend I ever had.' " And the note adds that this story came direct from Roscoe.

Page 220, the final sentence of the paragraph on Sir William Knighton was inserted only in proof.

Page 222, footnote 2 originally read: " An allusion to a well-known adventure with Mme. Georges, the actress."

Page 86, between paragraphs five and six: " One evening, Lord Grey, disgusted with the excesses of the French Revolution, exclaimed, ' I had rather live under an absolute despotism than in a democracy '; upon which Tooke said to him, ' Our ancestors at the Reformation were of the same way of thinking, for when they might have had purgatory, they chose hell-fire.' "

Page 227, between paragraphs two and three, the following is left undeleted in the proof, though it was

evidently cut out later: " Sir James Mackintosh gave the
following anecdote* to Lady Holland; where he got it, I
can't tell.—Queen Elizabeth one day surprised Raleigh
asleep in a chair. He told her that he had had a remarkable dream. She desired him to relate it. ' Methought,'
he said, ' I saw your majesty seated on your throne, and
attended by all your officers, when your royal father
entered the room. " Who is that? " he inquired of your
majesty. " That is Lord Leicester."—" Lord Leicester: I
know him not." " His name is Dudley."—" Oh, Dudley:
I remember I ordered his grandfather to be executed.
And who is that? " " Lord Burleigh! "—" Lord Burleigh:
I do not know him!" " His name is Cecil."—" Oh,
Cecil. Yes, his father was an attorney. And who is
that? " " An officer of my guard; his name is Raleigh."
—" Well, *he* really looks like a gentleman." ' "

Dyce's note : This is not the only historical anecdote which
Mr. Rogers used to repeat after Sir James; but the reader,
I presume, will be satisfied with a single specimen of these
ingenious fictions.

———

The manuscript corrections on D. 3403 are of less
interest. Apart from the correction to the footnote on
page 135, which I have made in the text, they consist only
in the addition of two parallel passages. The first of these
relates to the observation on page 18, " I sometimes wonder
how a man can ever be cheerful," etc., and is as follows:
Madame du Deffand says;

' Vivre sans aimer la vie ne fait pas désirer sa fin, et
même ne diminue guères la crainte de la perdre; *ceux de
qui la vie est heureuse ont un point de vue bien triste, ils ont la
certitude qu'elle finira.*'

Letters to H. Walpole, vol. iv. 55.

The other, on the passage on page 147, " What comes
from the heart goes to the heart," comments:
Compare Thomson;

' to the heart,
Pour'd ardent forth in eloquence unbid,
The heart attends.'

Poem to the memory of the Lord Talbot.

INDEX

INDEX

MADE AND PRINTED IN GREAT BRITAIN
AT THE CHAPEL RIVER PRESS
ANDOVER, HANTS
10.52